Art Catalogue

Ruth Velikovsky Sharon, PhD

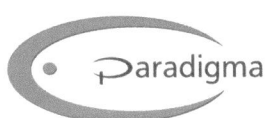

If there is interest or inquiry about any of the works in this catalogue, please contact:

> Dr. Ruth Velikovsky Sharon
> 50 Deer Path
> Princeton, New Jersey 08540
> USA
> email: ruthvsharonphd@verizon.net
> telephone: 1-609-921-0959
> cell: 609-731-0261

Copyright © 2010 by   Ruth Velikovsky Sharon, Ph.D.

Internet: www.ruthvelikovskysharon.com
e-mail: ruthvsharonphd@verizon.net

All rights reserved. No part of this book may be reproduced or transmitted in any form or by any means, electronic or mechanical, including photocopying, recording, or by any information storage and retrieval system, without permission in writing from the copyright owner, except by reviewers who may quote brief passages to be printed in a magazine or newspaper.

Photographs: Mark Czajkowski

Published by   Paradigma Ltd.
Internet: www.paradigma-publishing.com
e-mail: info@paradigma-publishing.com

ISBN 978-1-906833-03-9

Ruth Velikovsky Sharon, PhD

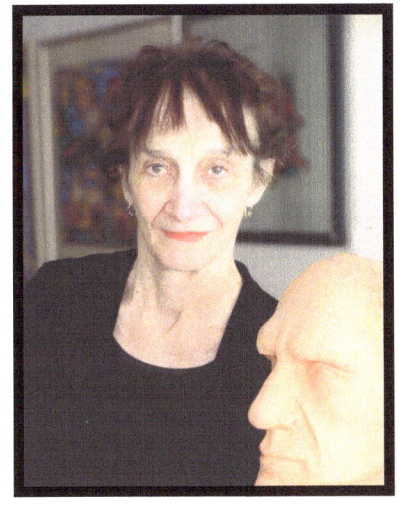

Dr. Ruth Velikovsky Sharon learned at the desk of her distinguished father, Dr. Immanuel Velikovsky, a prominent psychiatrist and eminent man of science whose genius engaged even the mind of his friend and contemporary, Albert Einstein.

At the same time, sitting in the room with her mother's (Elis Velikovsky) works, listening to Mozart, she had herself inspired artistically.

Dr. Sharon received B.A and M.A. degrees from New York University and a Ph.D. from the Union Institute and University. She is a graduate of the Center for Modern Psychoanalytic Studies and a certified psychoanalyst.

She taught arts and crafts at the Sharon Studio in Princeton from 1955 to 1974, which enjoyed a well deserved reputation for originating new concepts of teaching in this field to children, with emphasis on liberating creativity and undisturbed self-expression.

She has exhibited in central New Jersey, including the New Jersey State Museum, and also in New York in The Pen and Brush.

She works with pen and india ink, with watercolors, on leather, silk, linen, burlap and blotter paper. Her favorite themes are the violin (because of her mother), Jerusalem (where she was born) and birds (simply because of their shape).

Her One-Woman Shows:

    1972 Artisan, Princeton, New Jersey

    1974 The Suzuki Gallery Kingston, New Jersey

    1976 Gallery 100 Princeton, New Jersey

    1987 The Pen and Brush, New York, New York

    1987 The Full House, Kingston, New Jersey

    1990 Williams Collection New Visions Gallery, Kingston, New Jersey

    1992 The Jewish Center, Sponsored by the Williams Collection, Princeton, New Jersey

    1998 The Verdge, Princeton, New Jersey

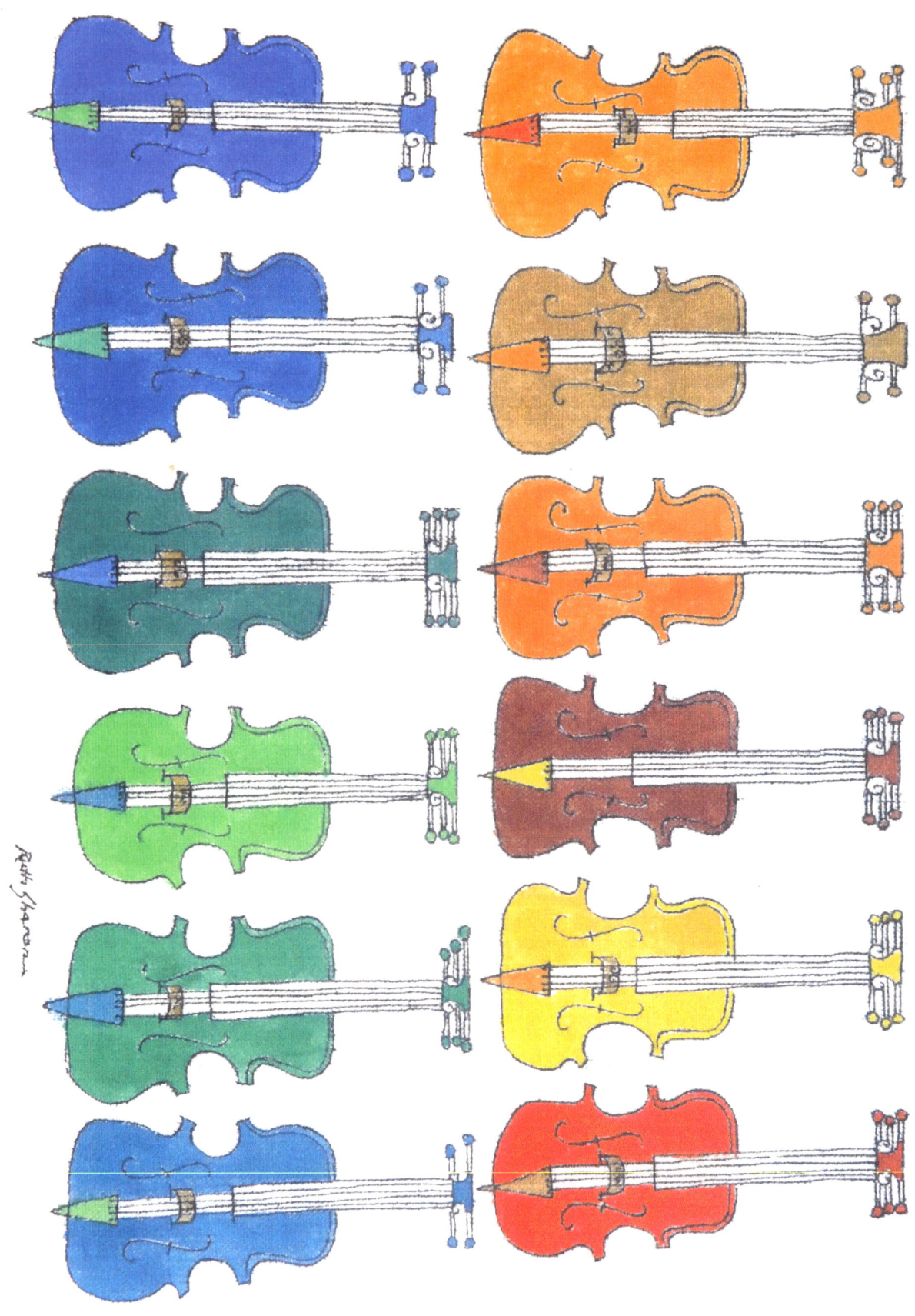

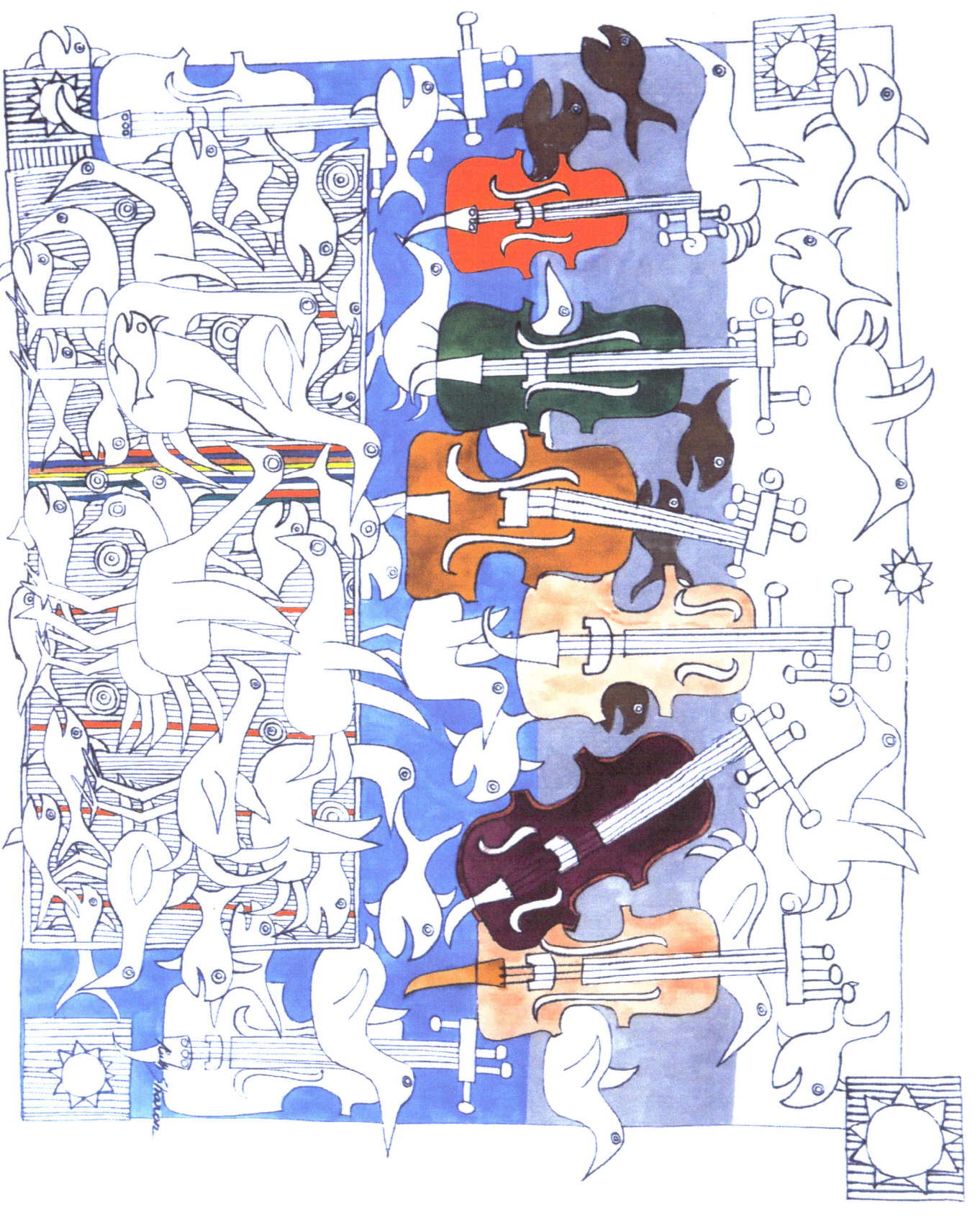

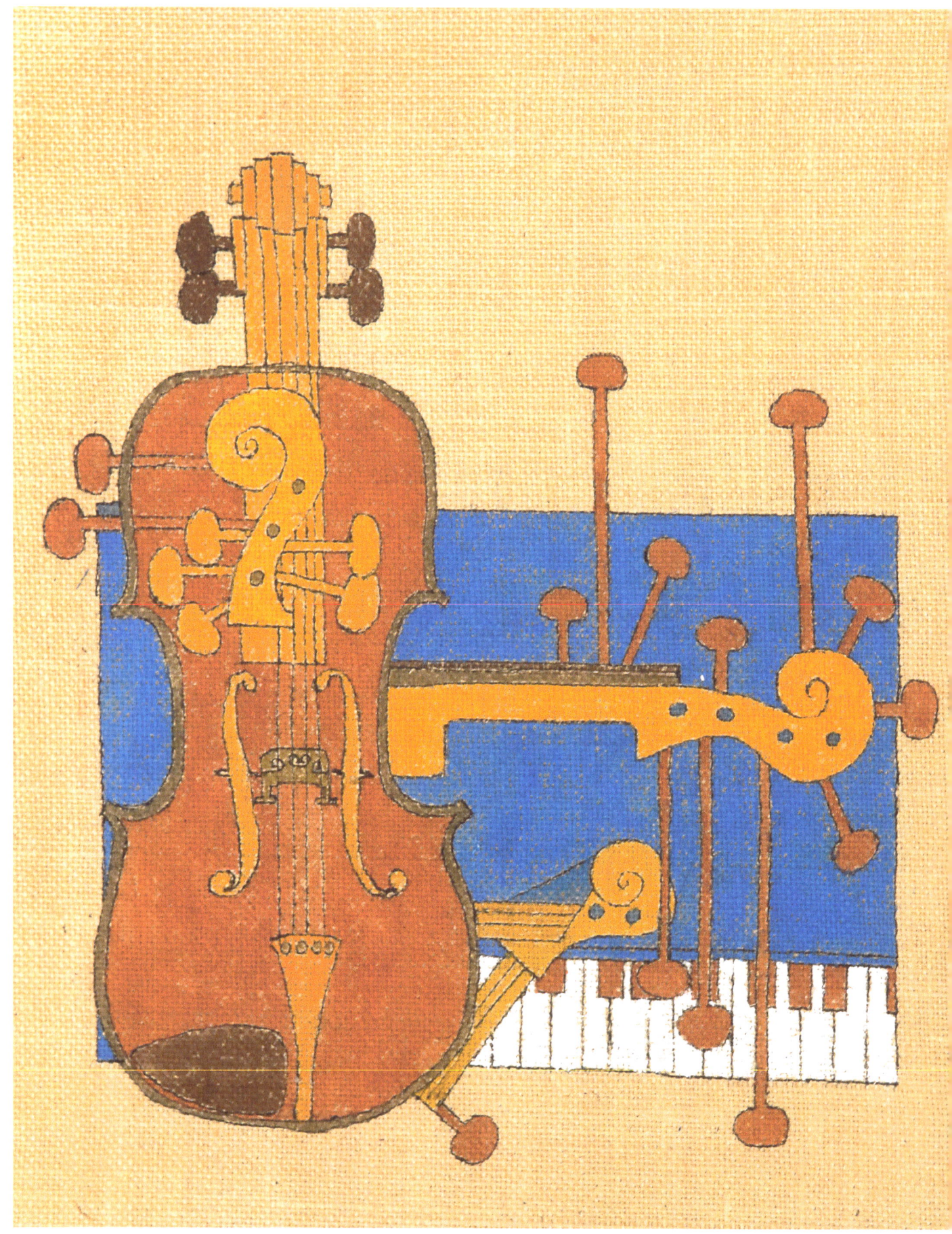

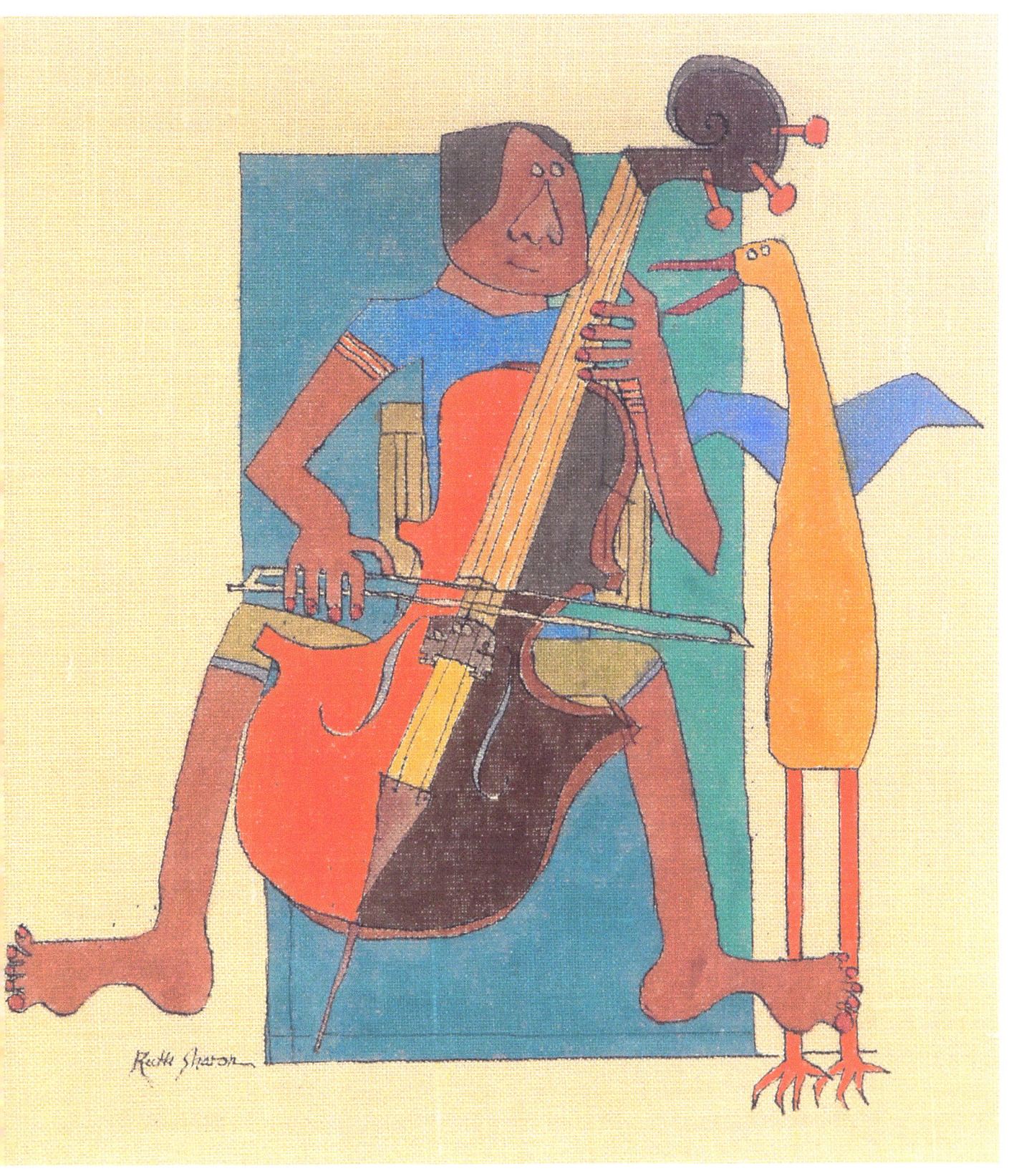

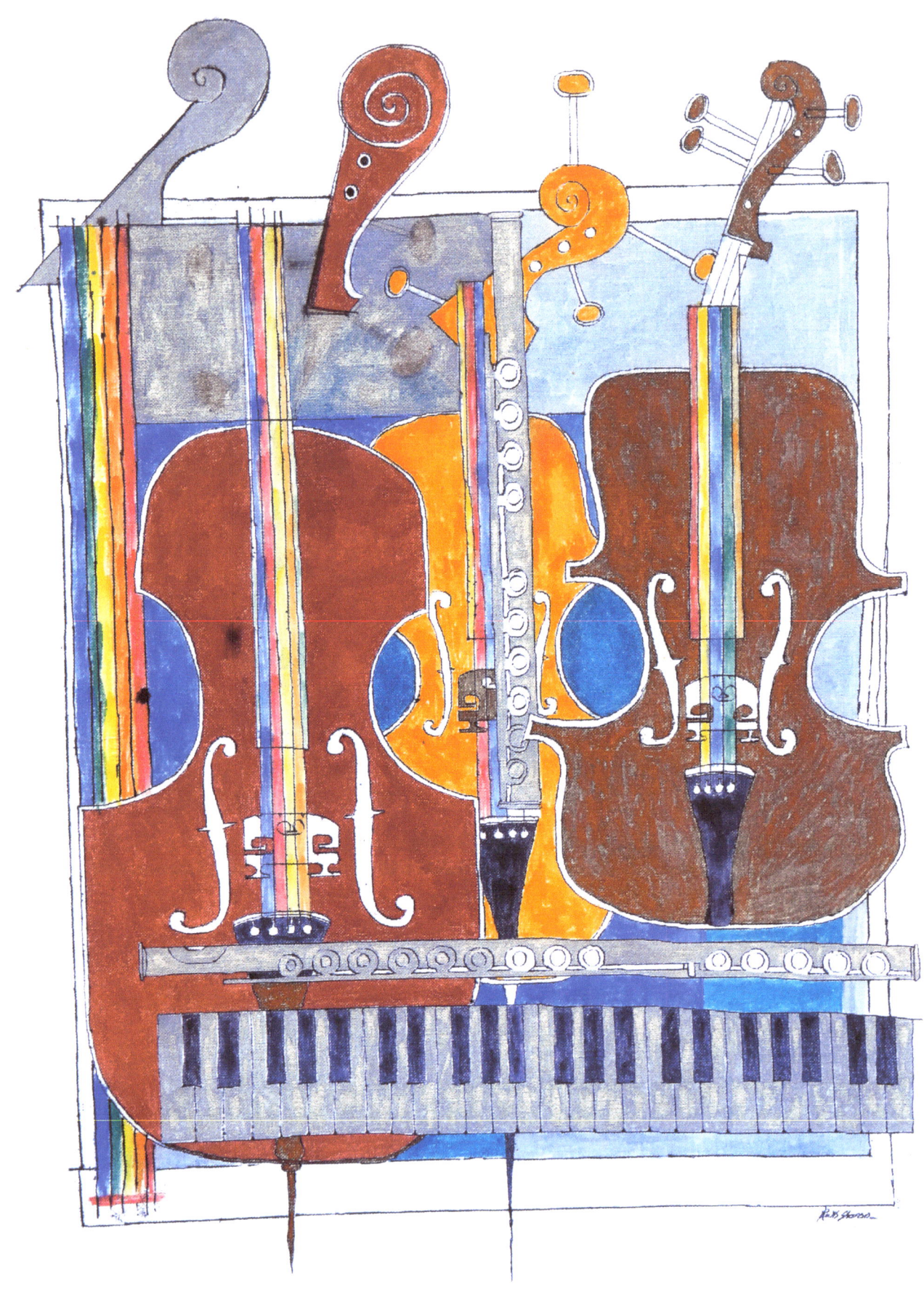

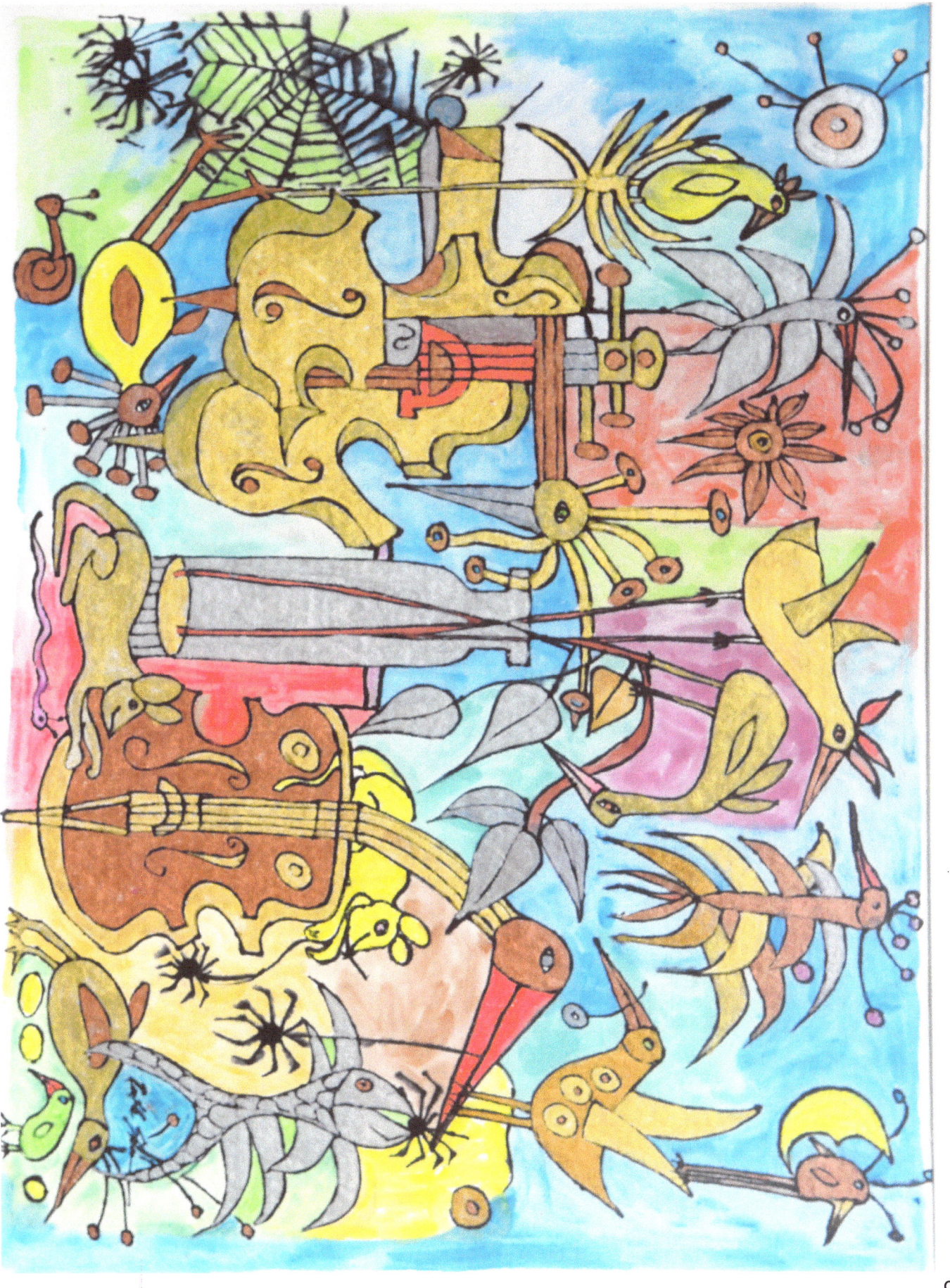

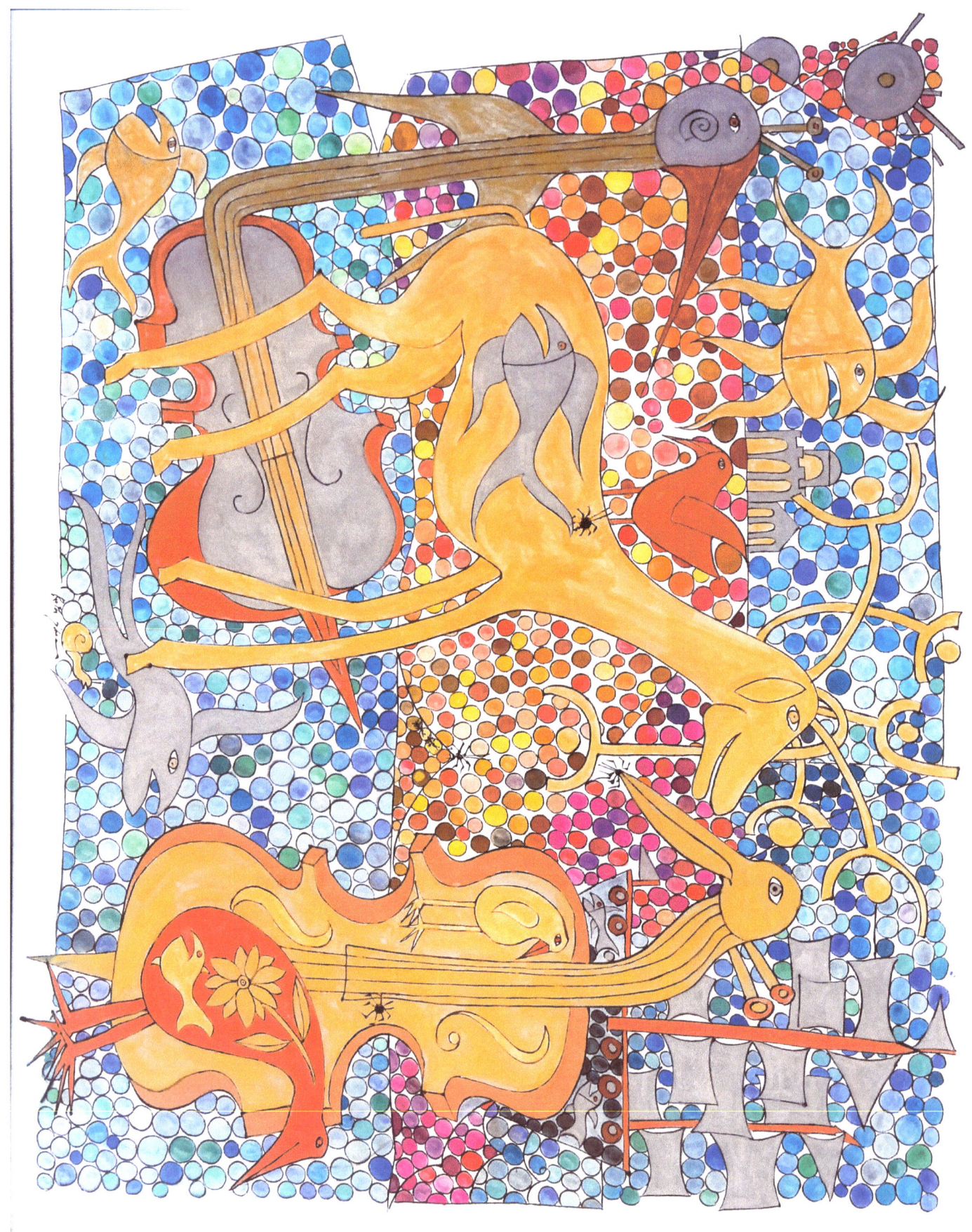

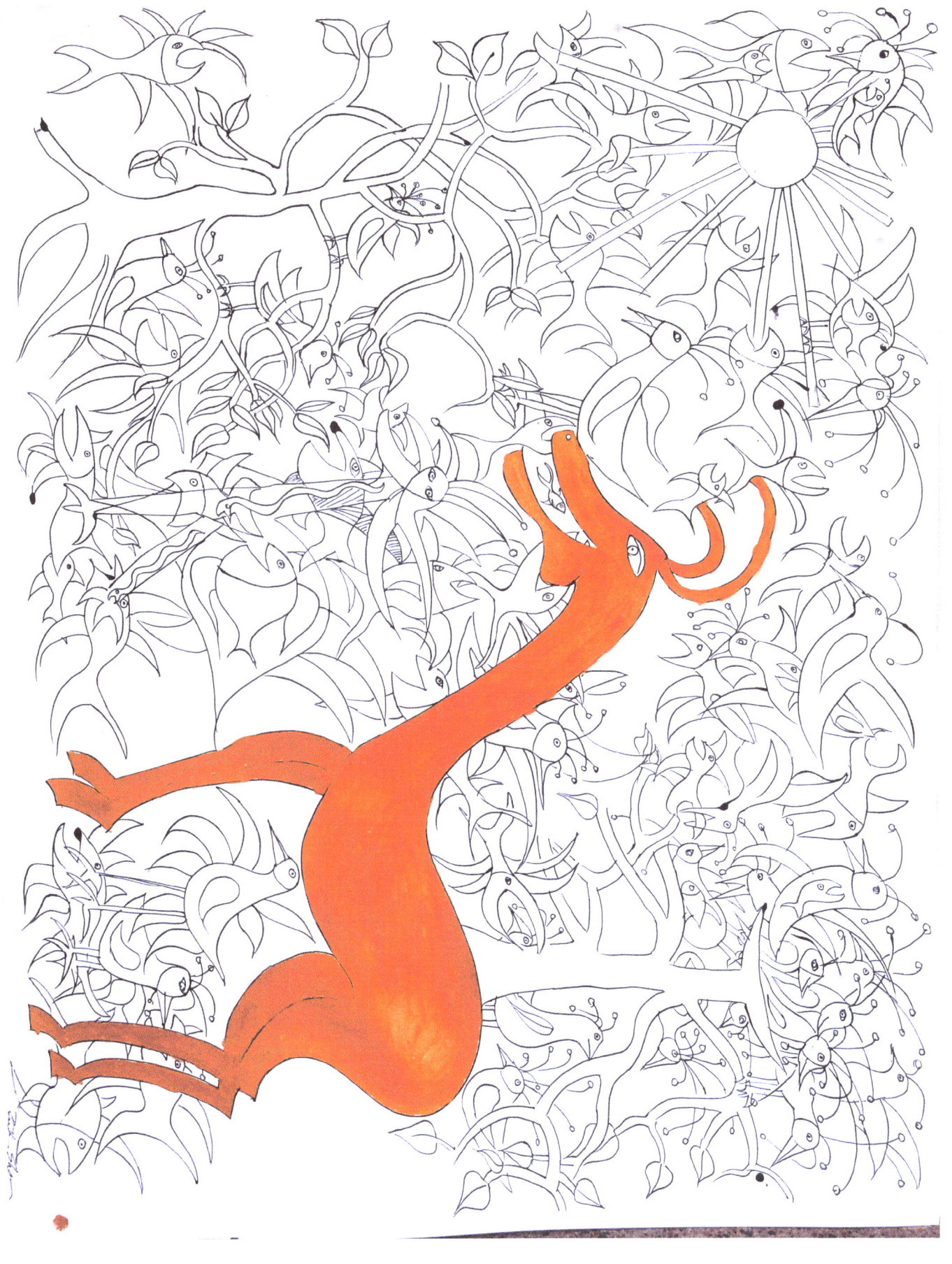

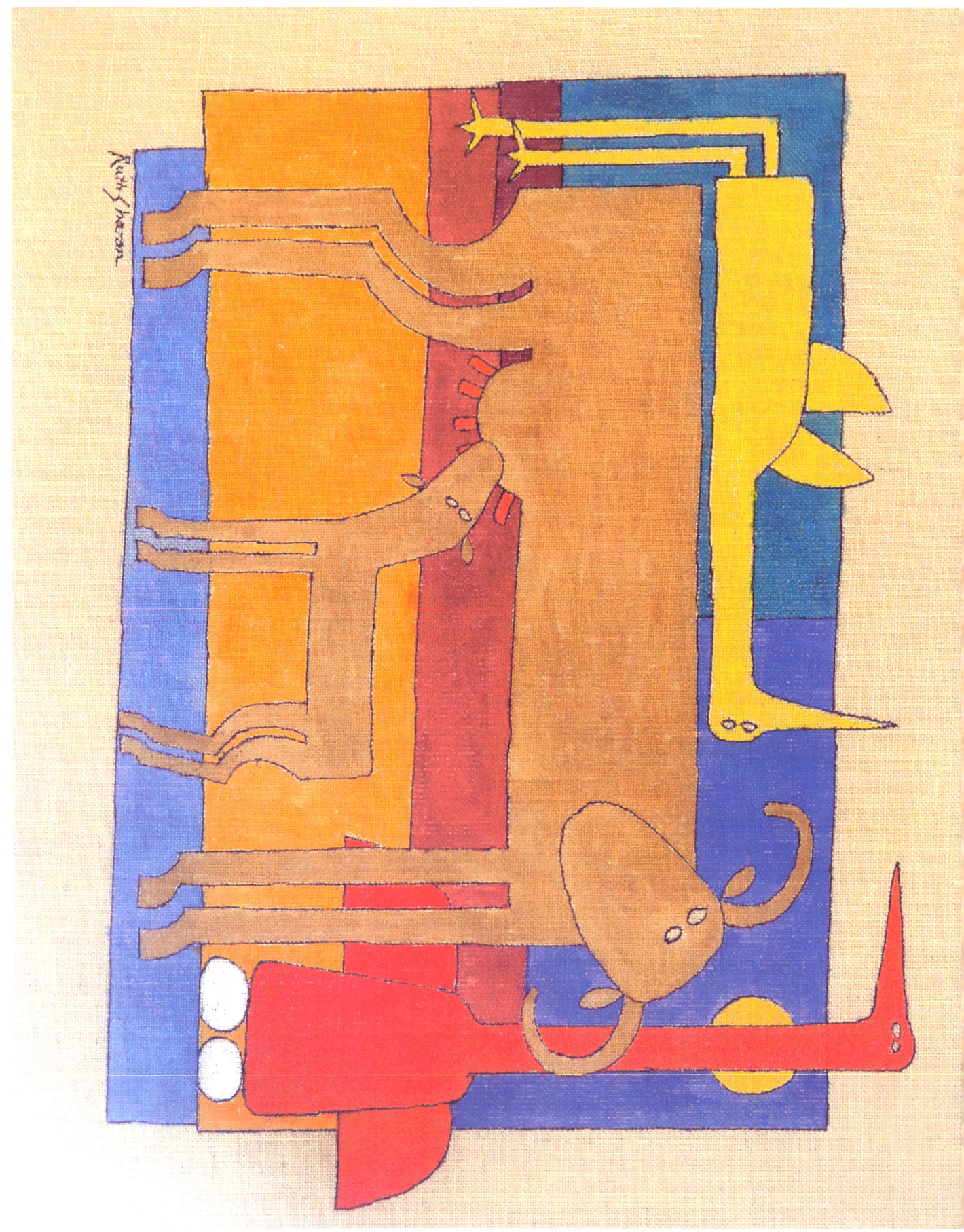

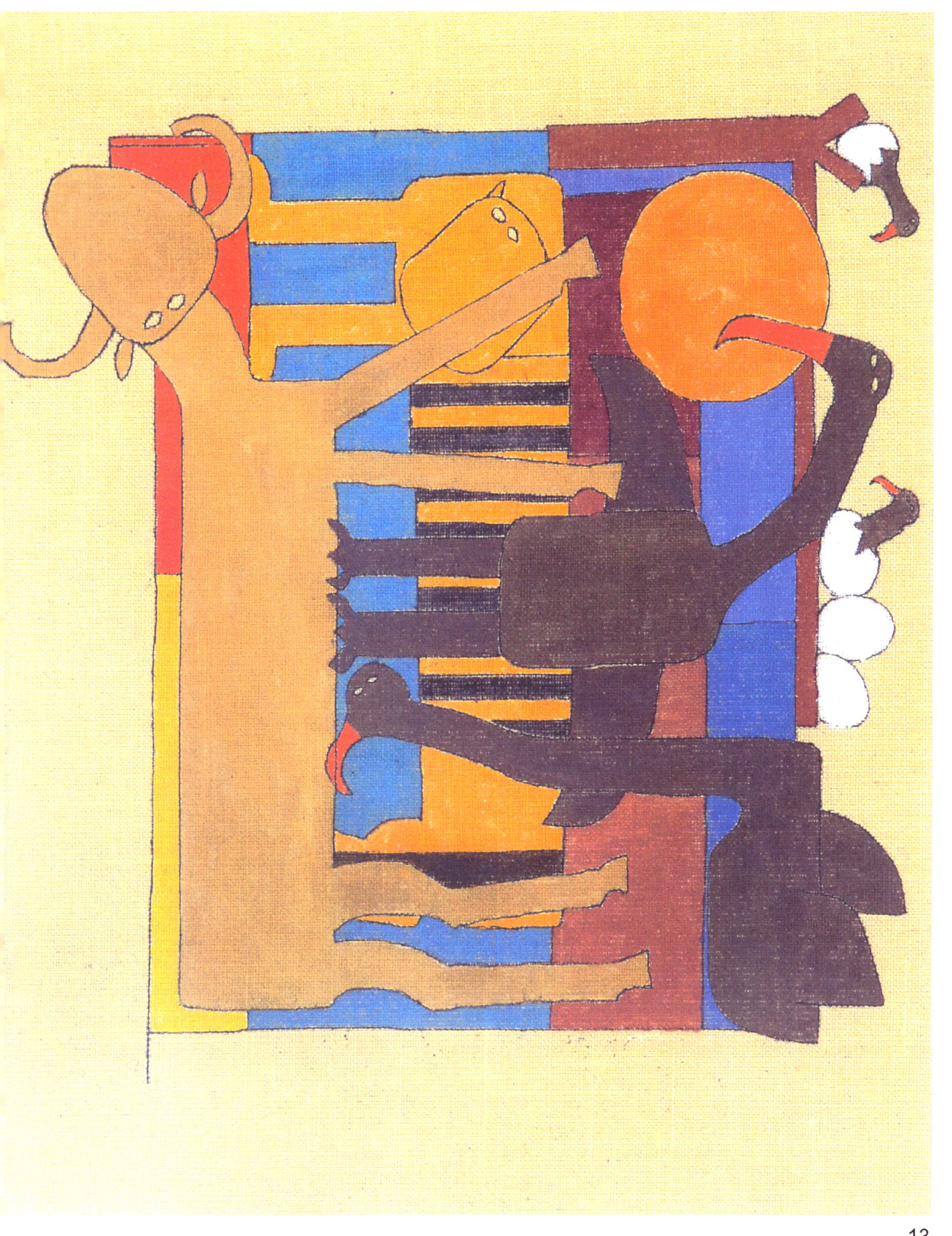

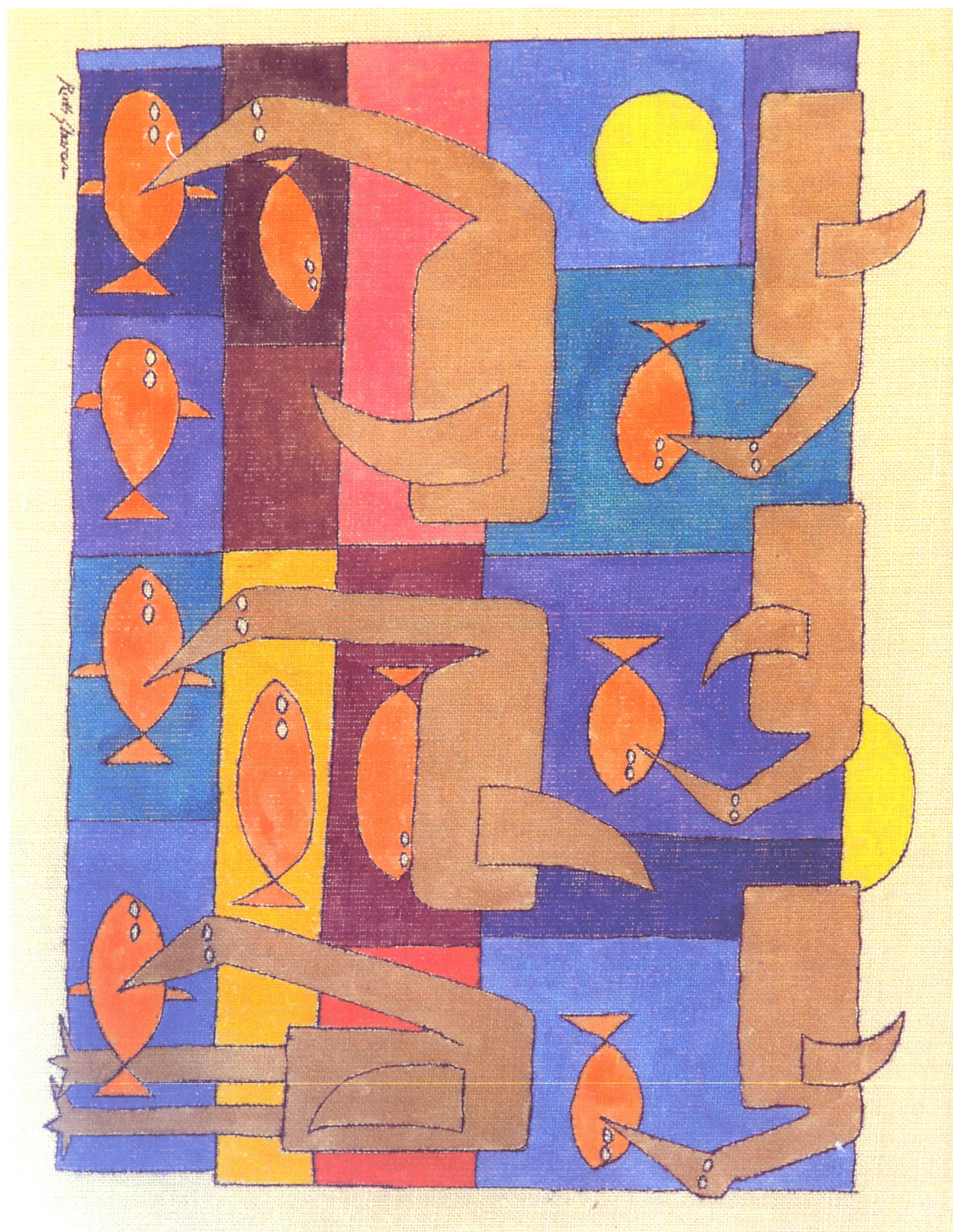

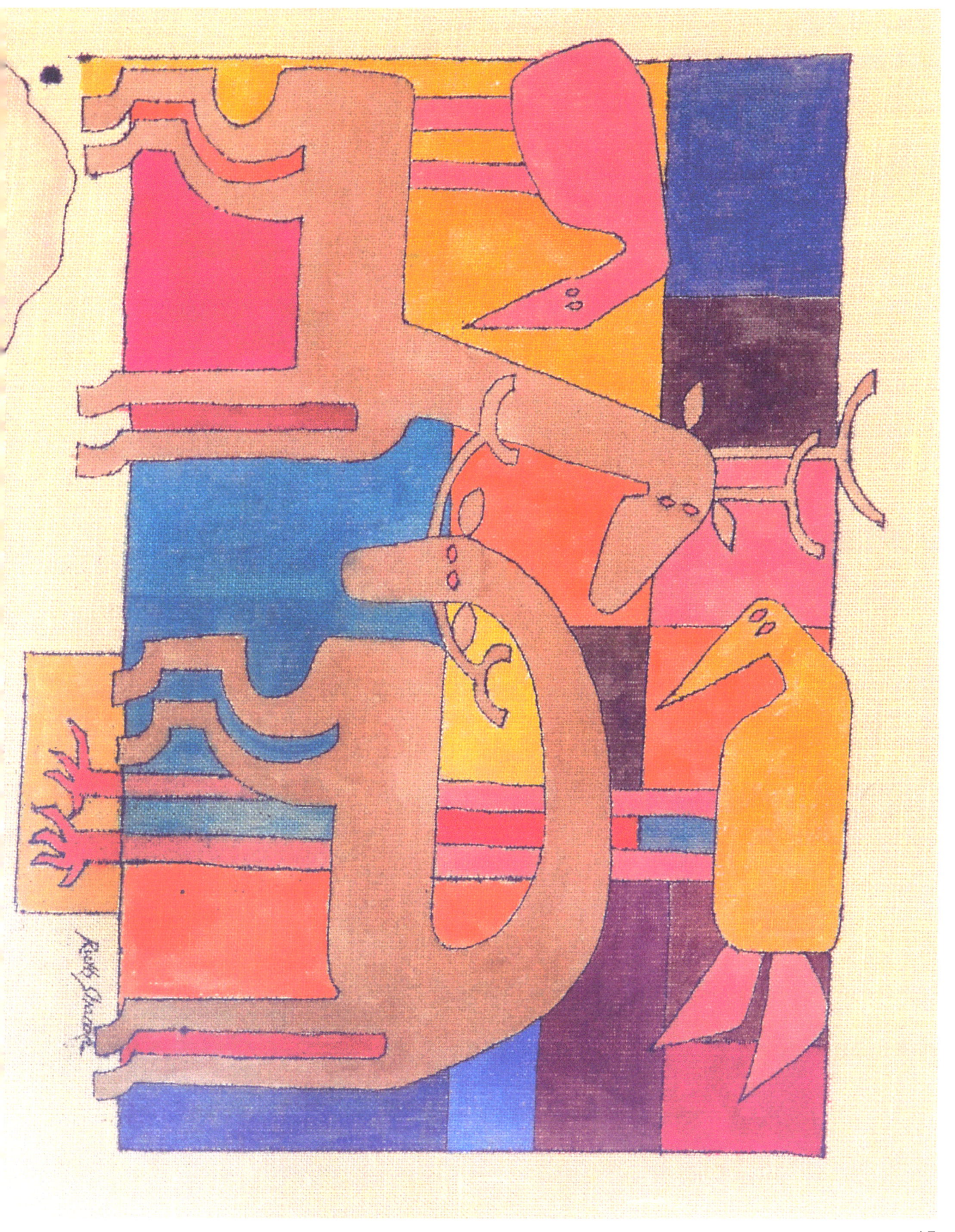

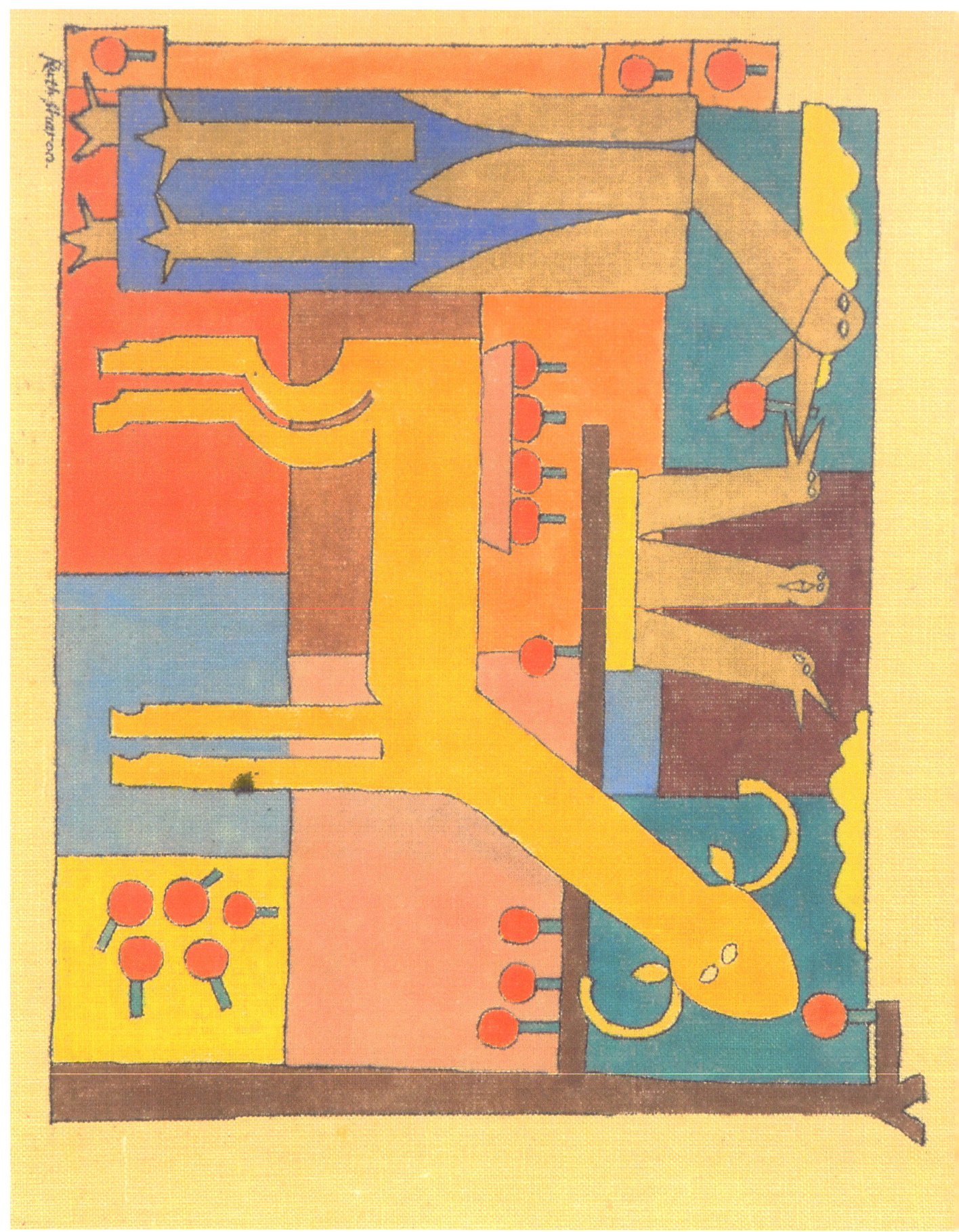

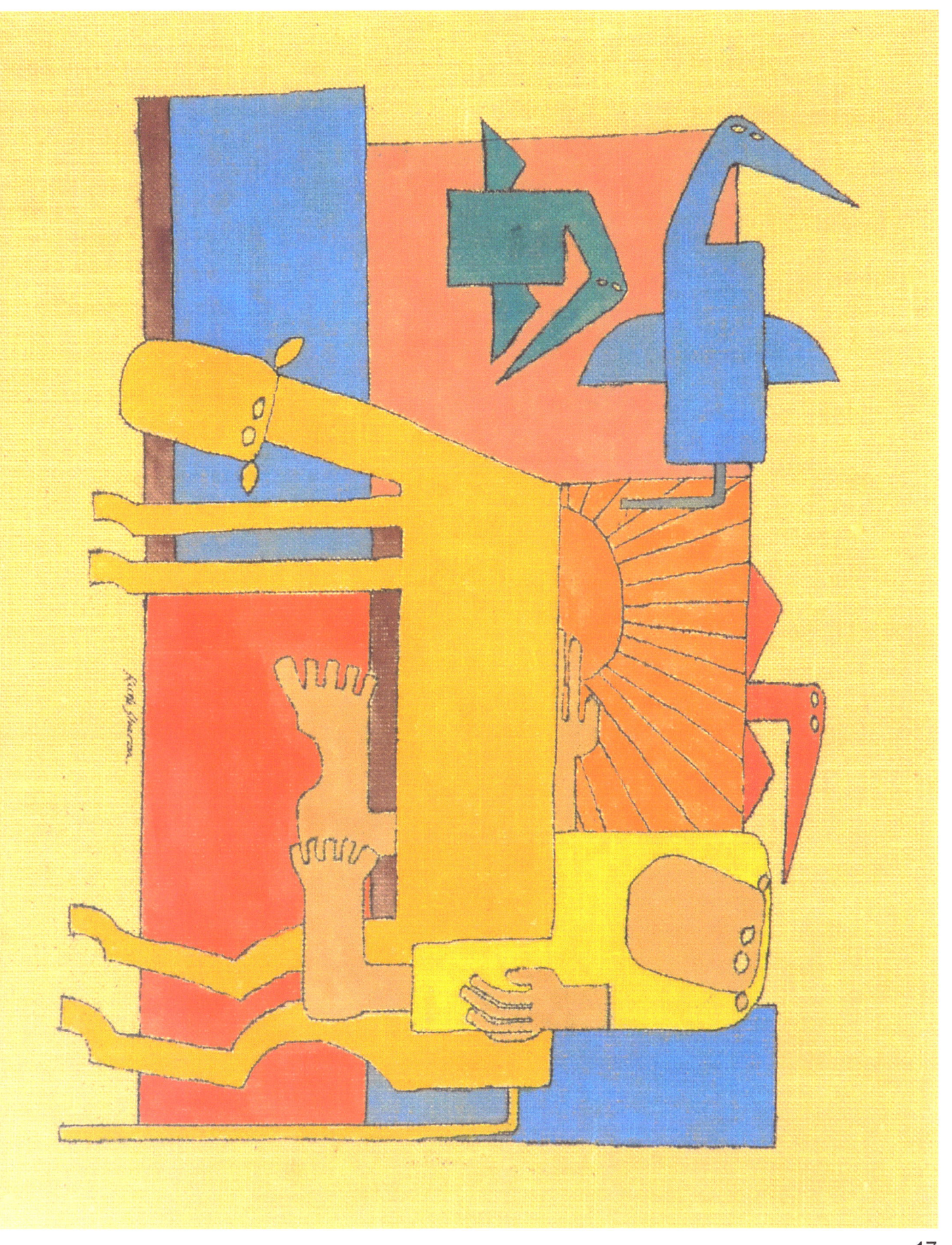

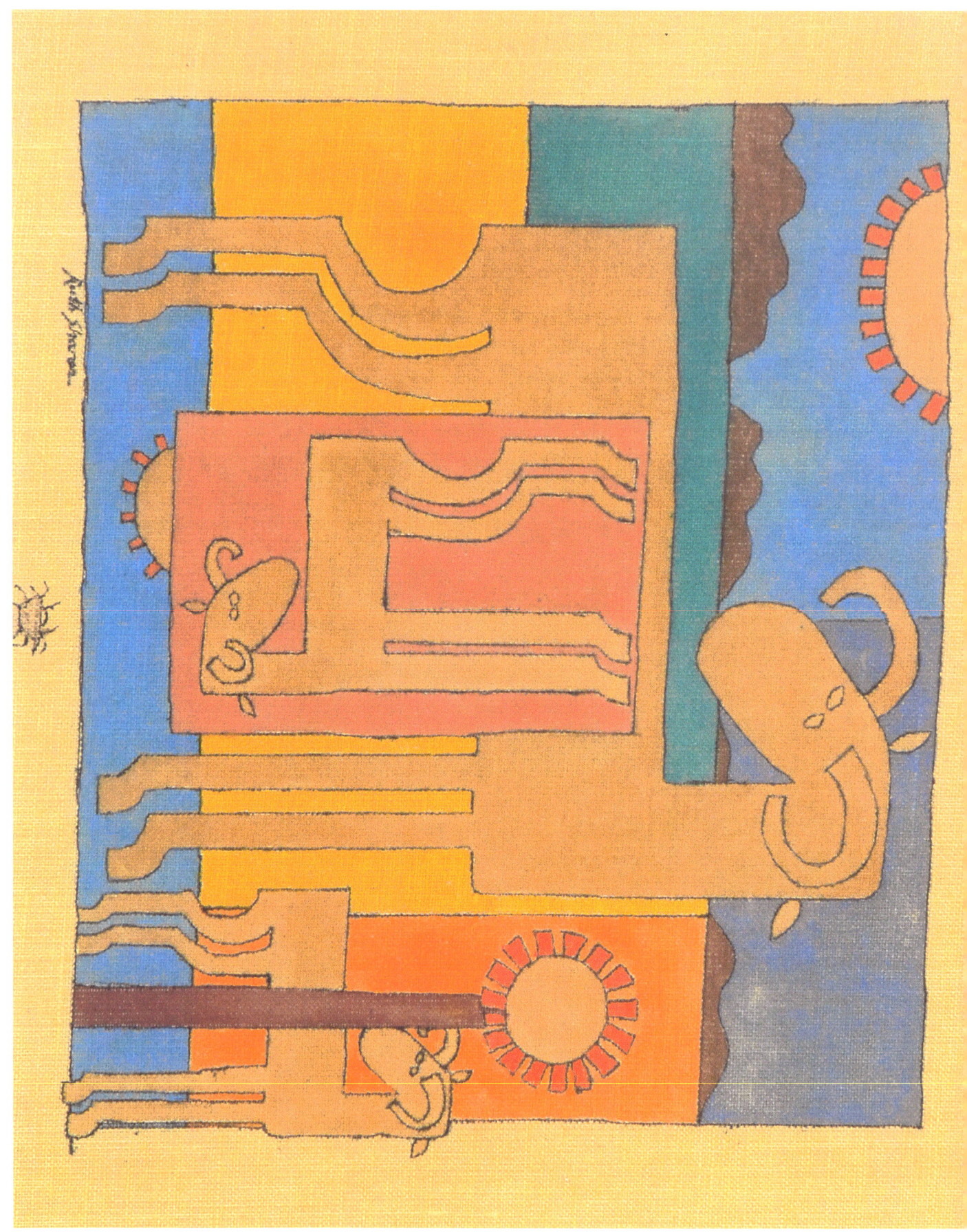

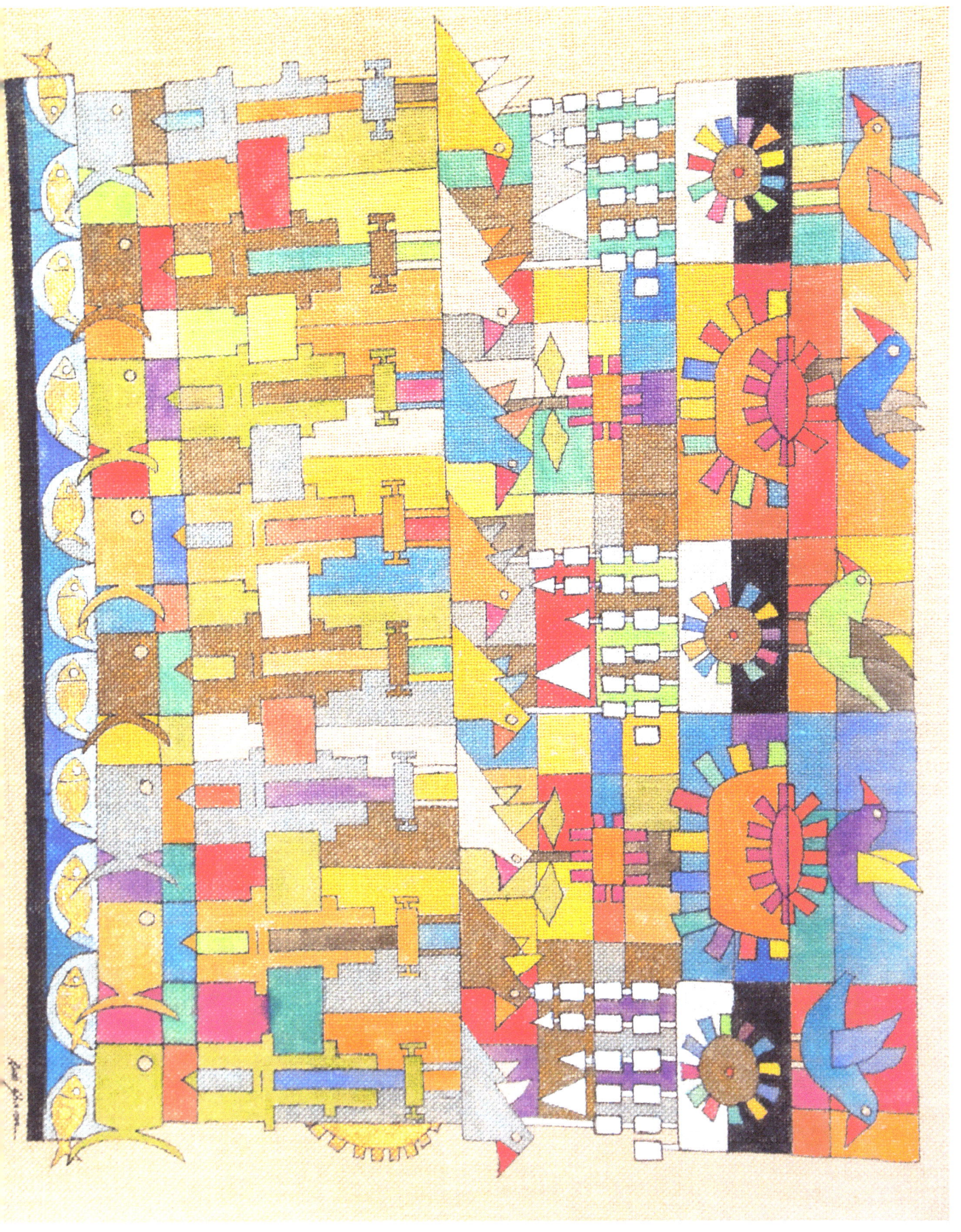

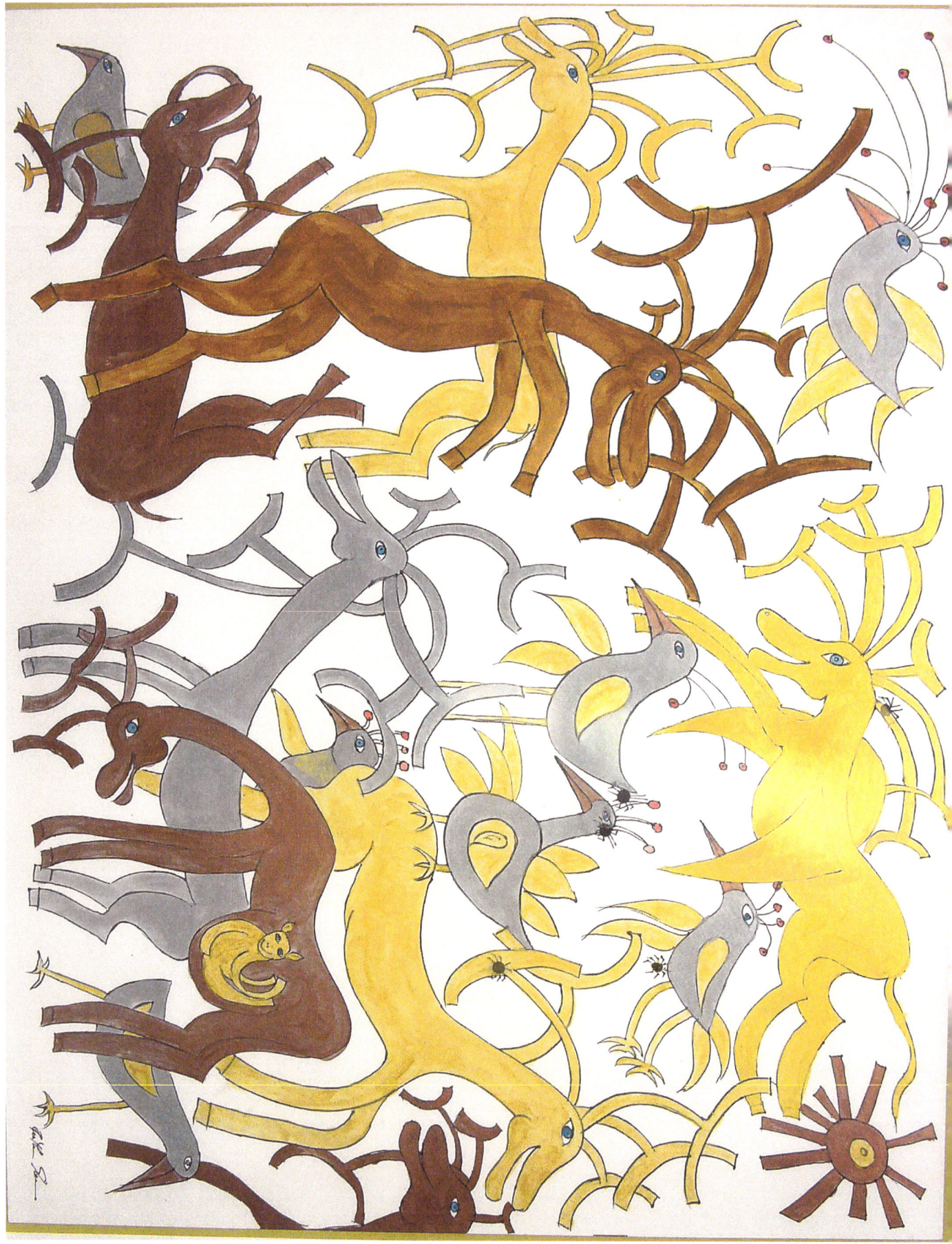

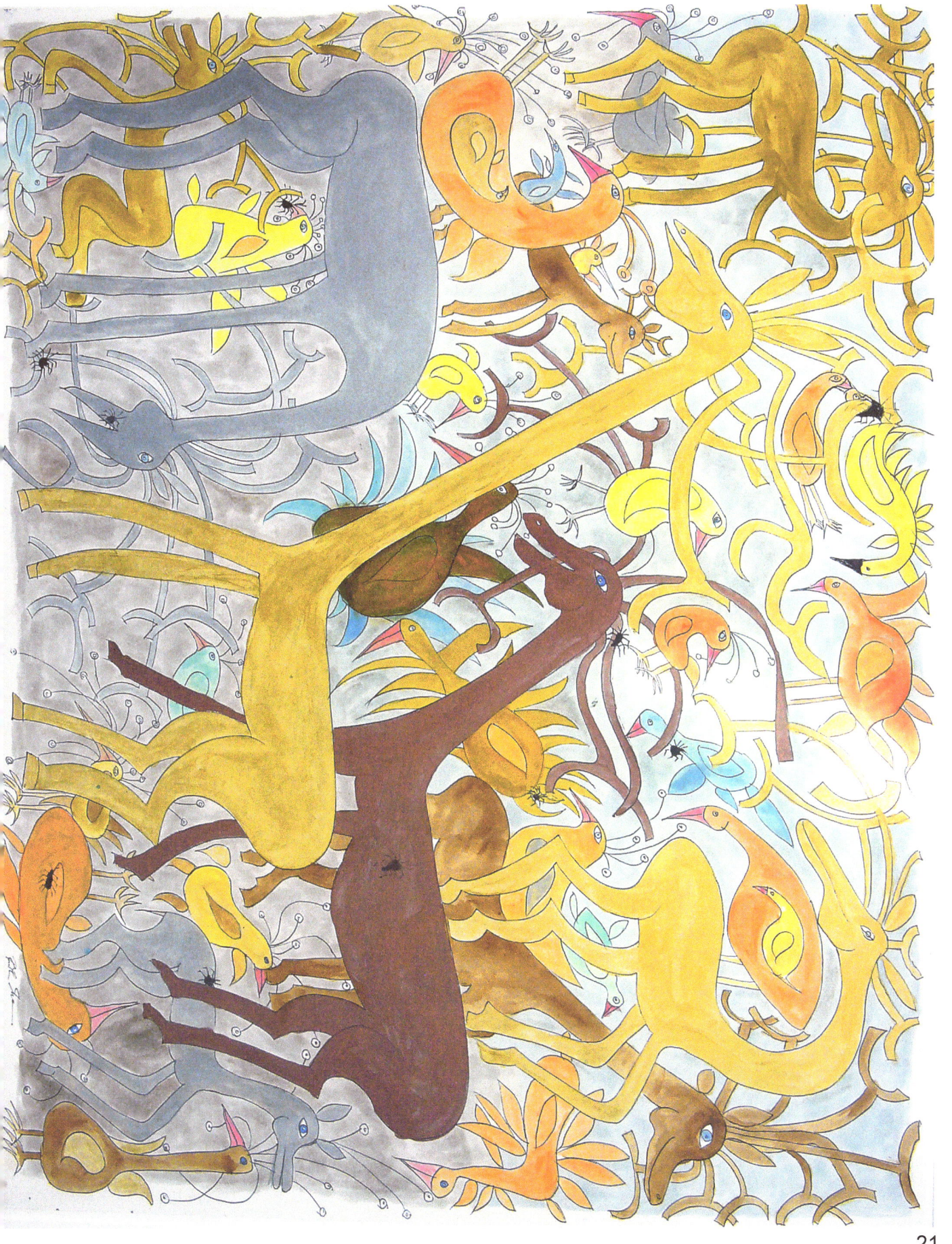

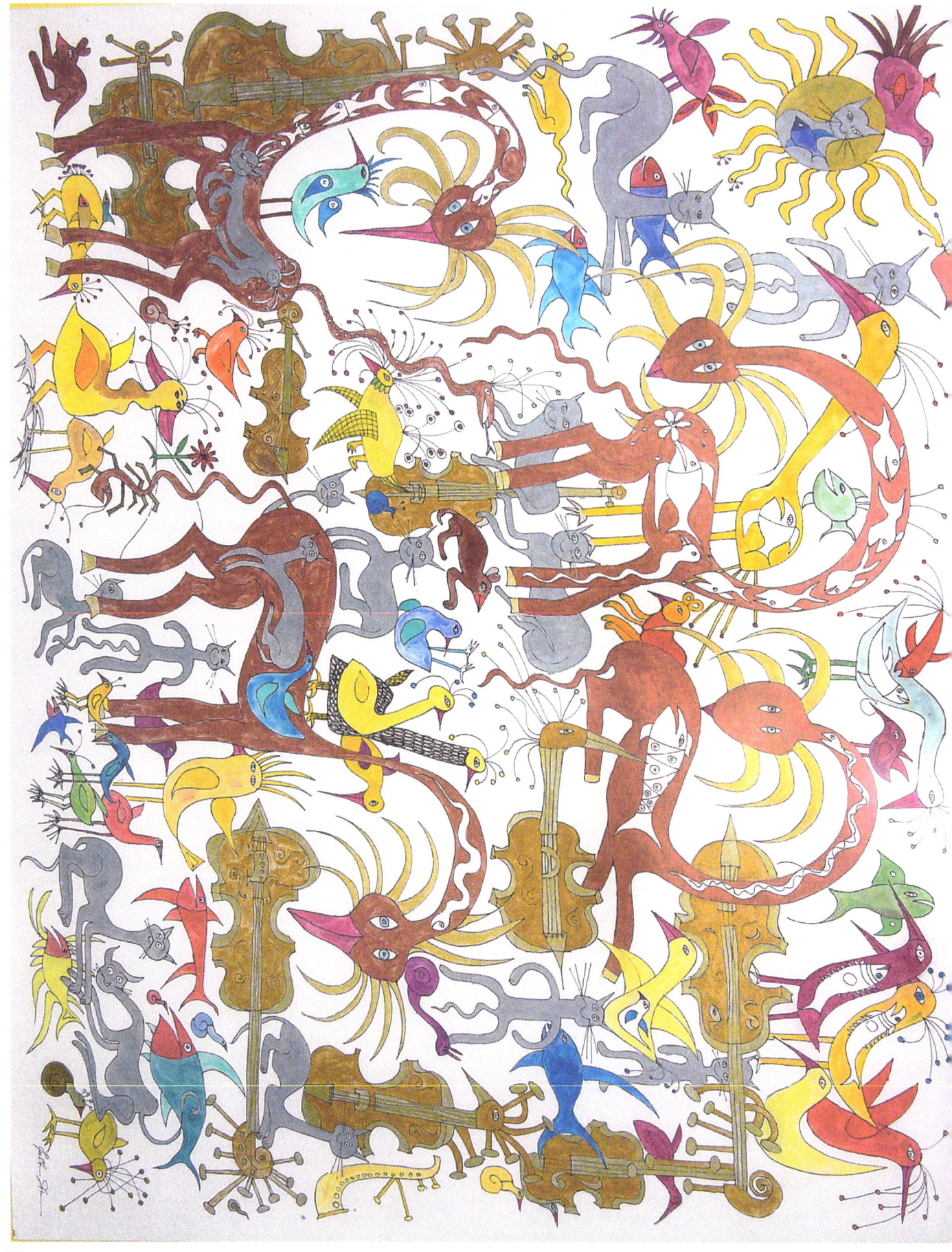

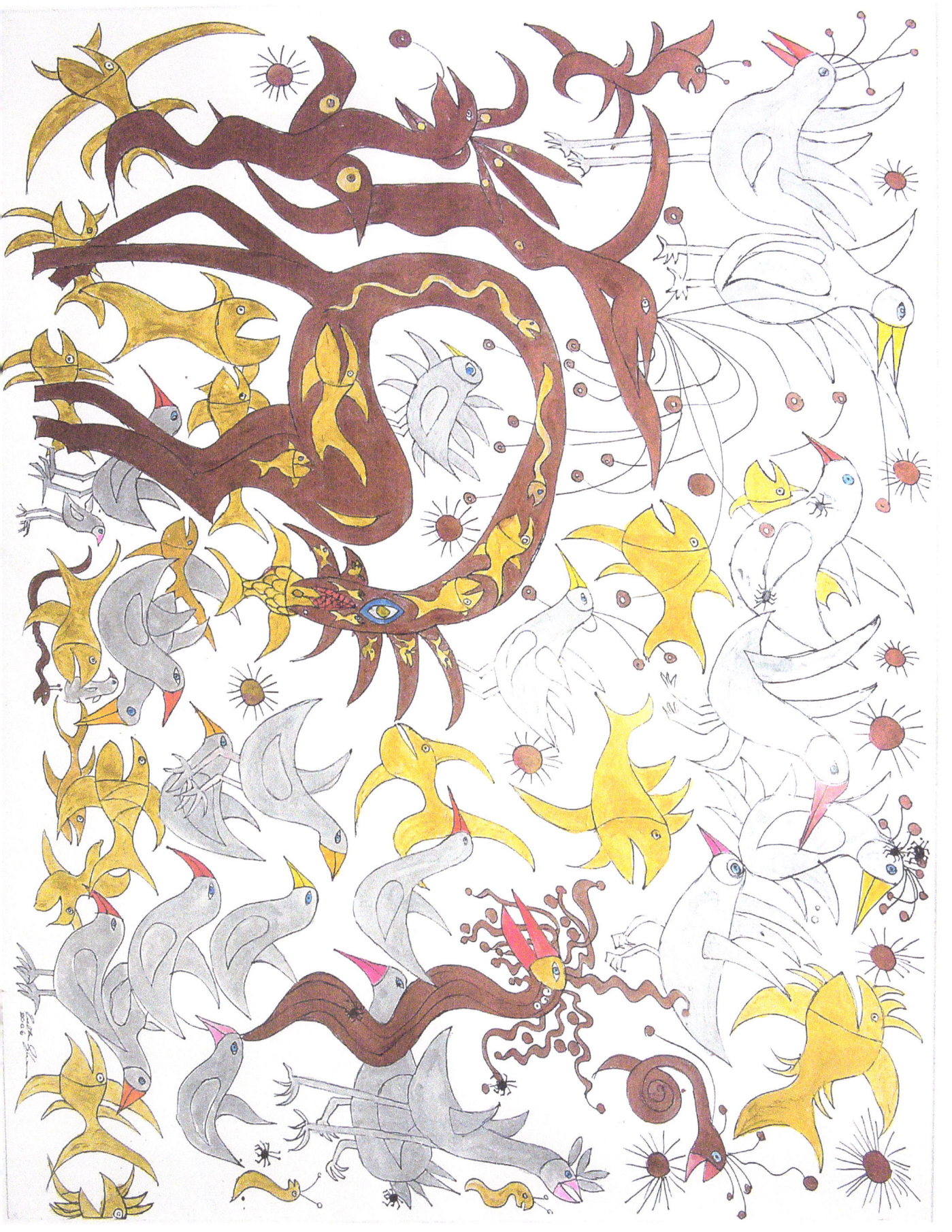

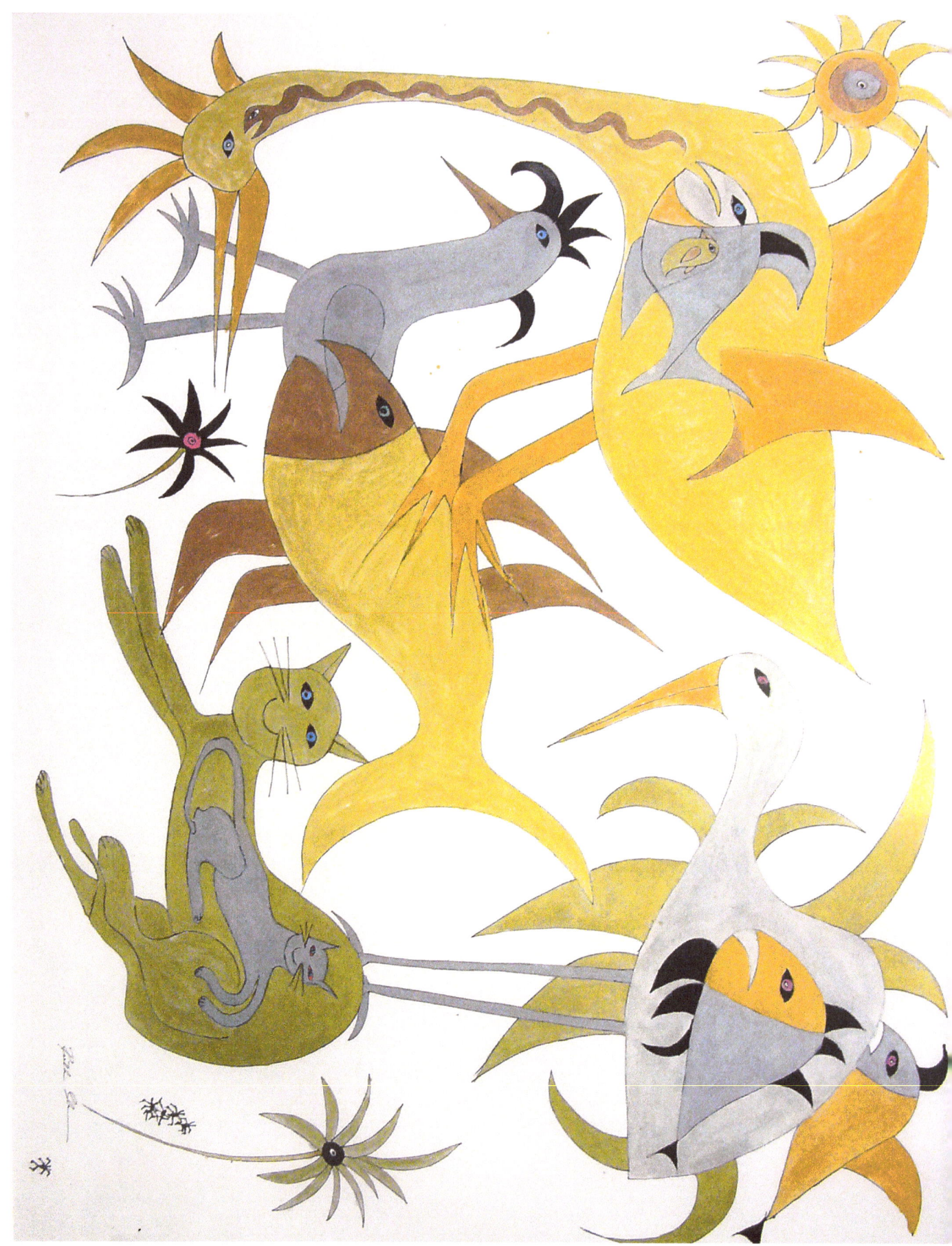

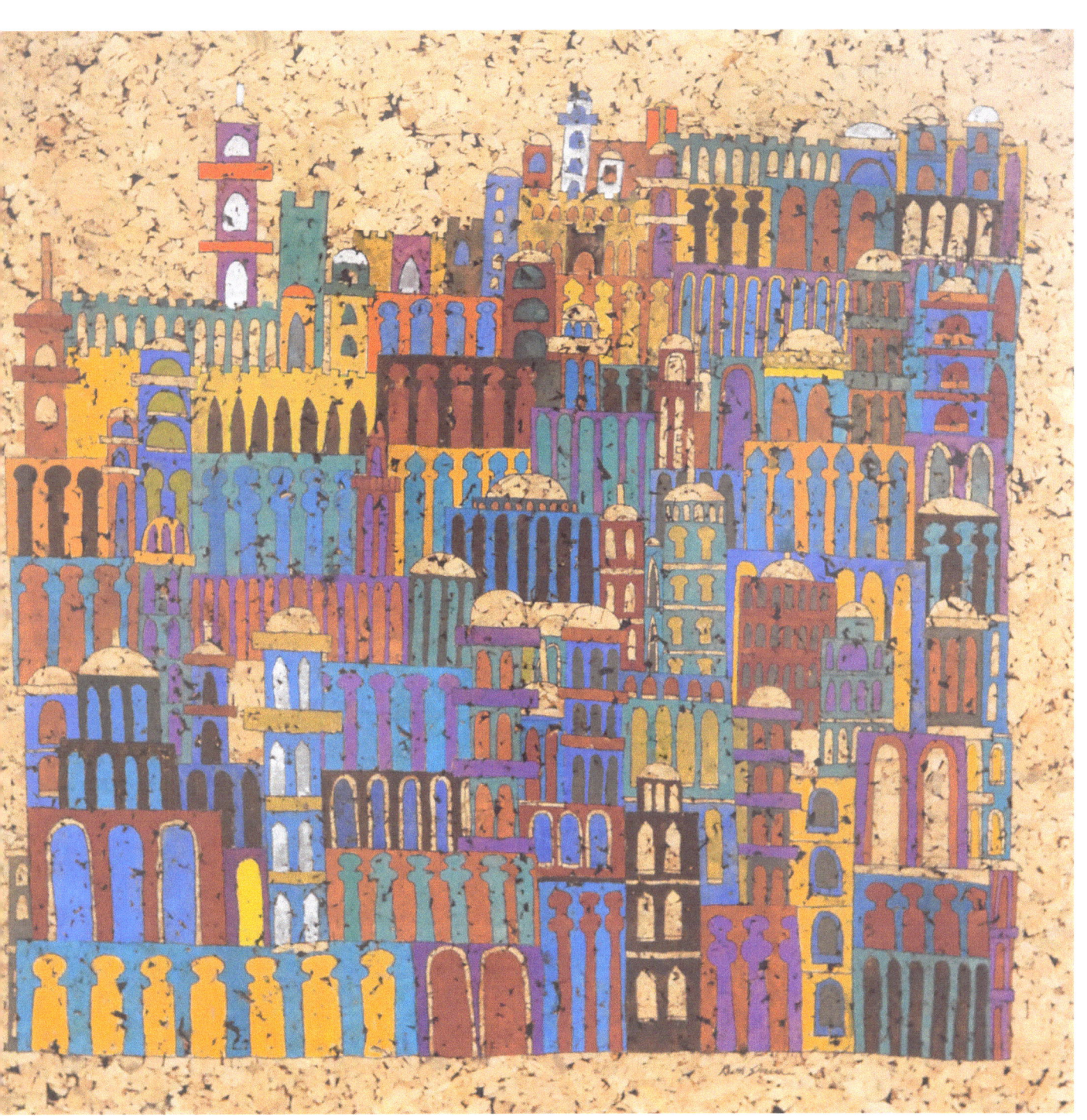

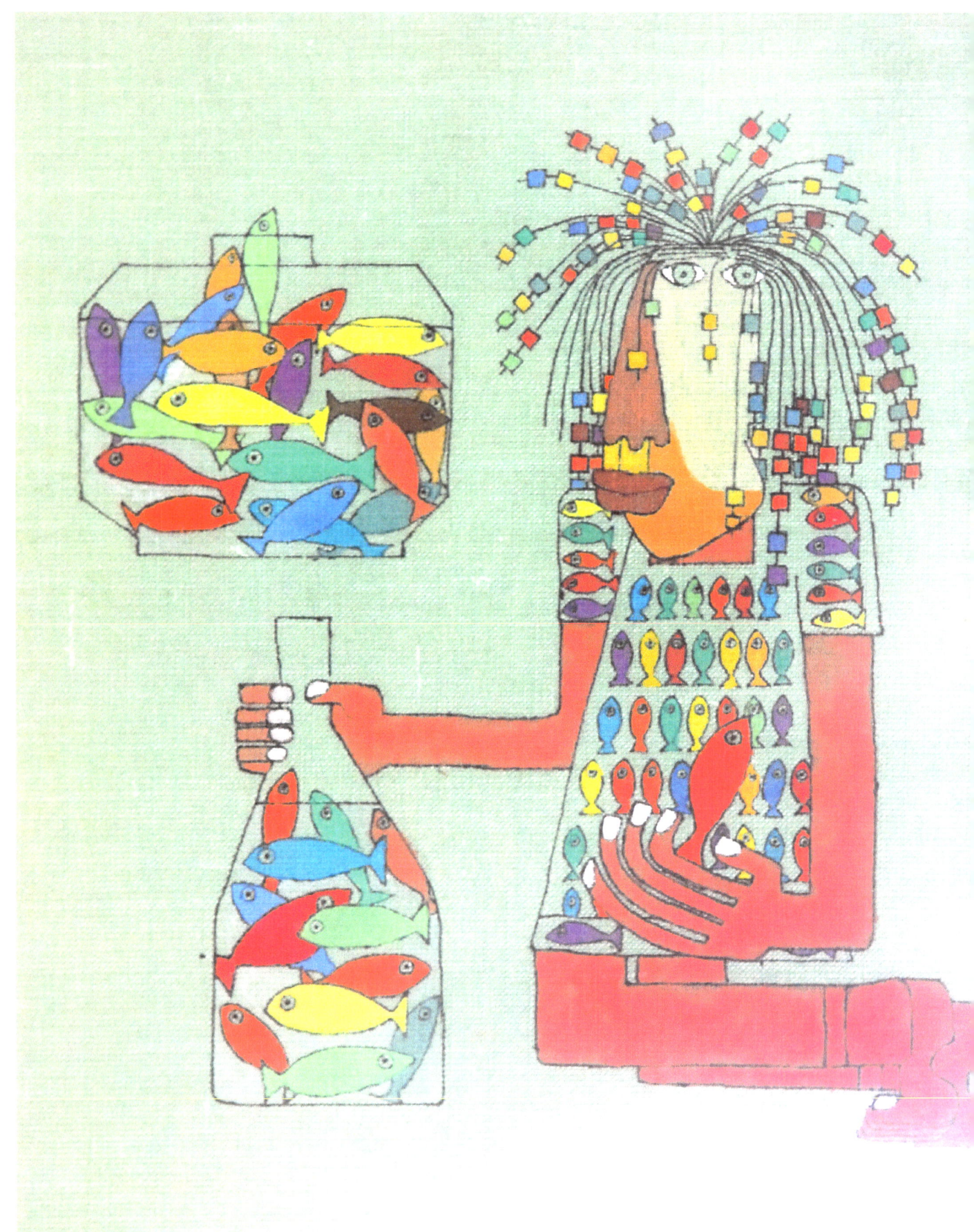

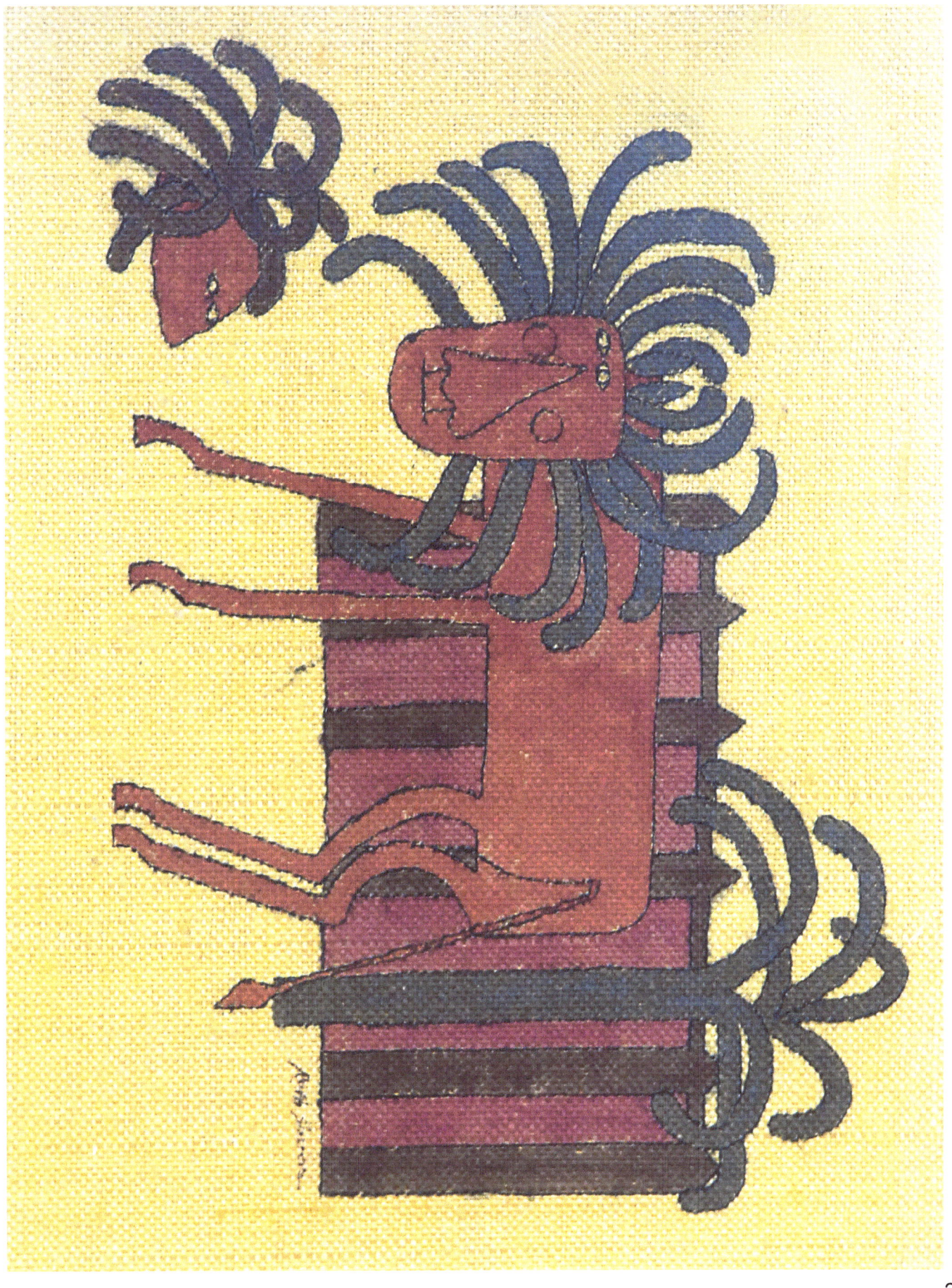

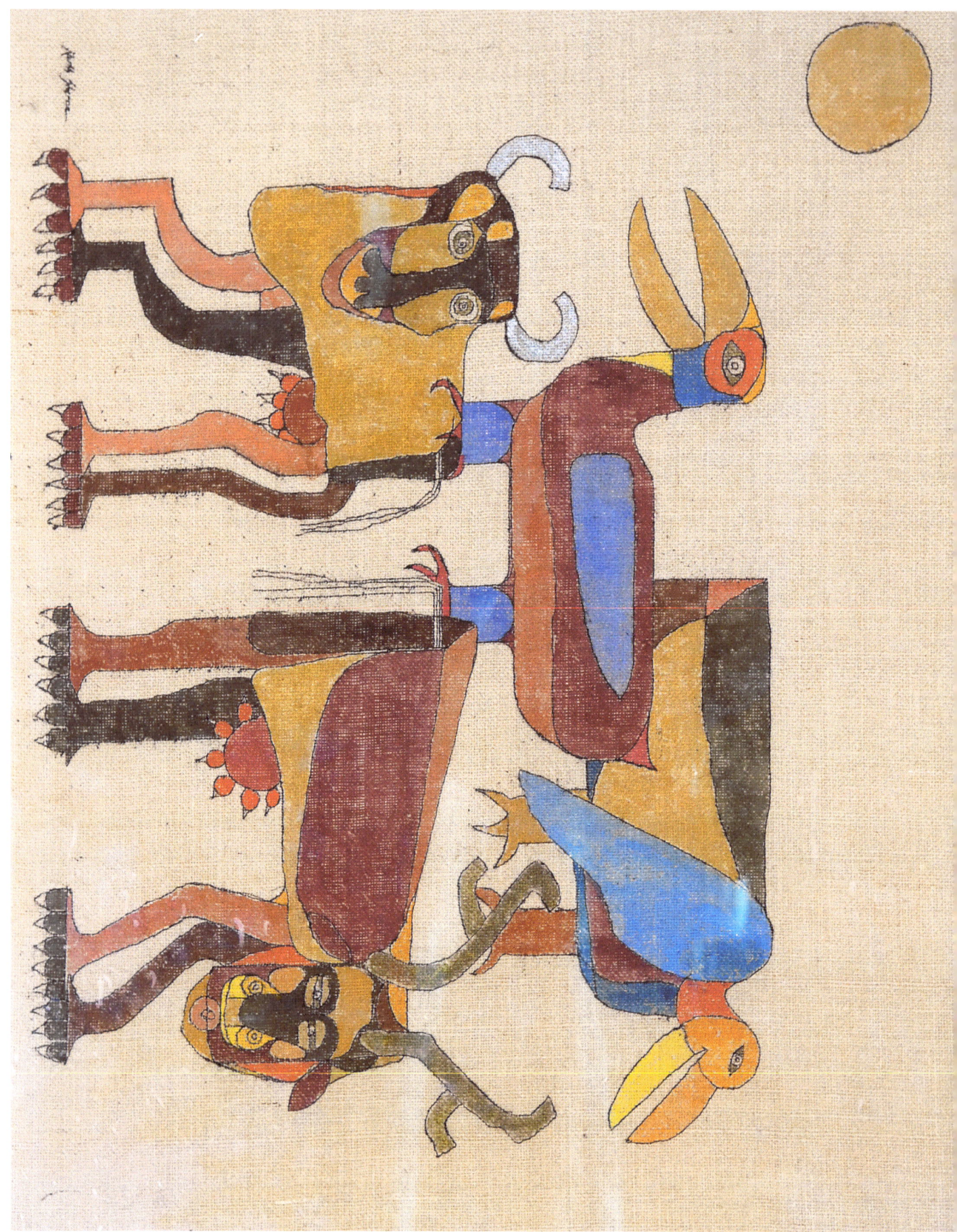

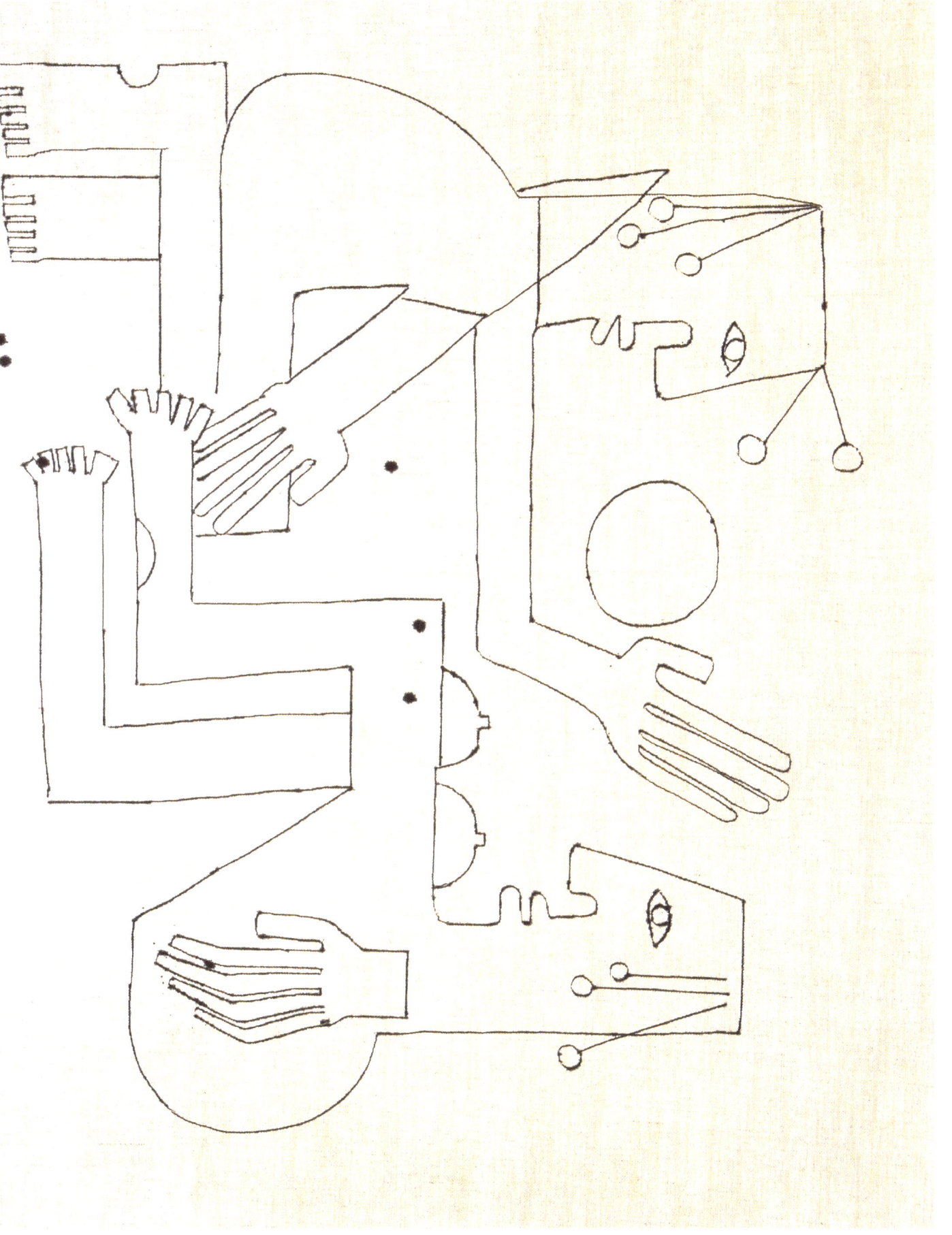

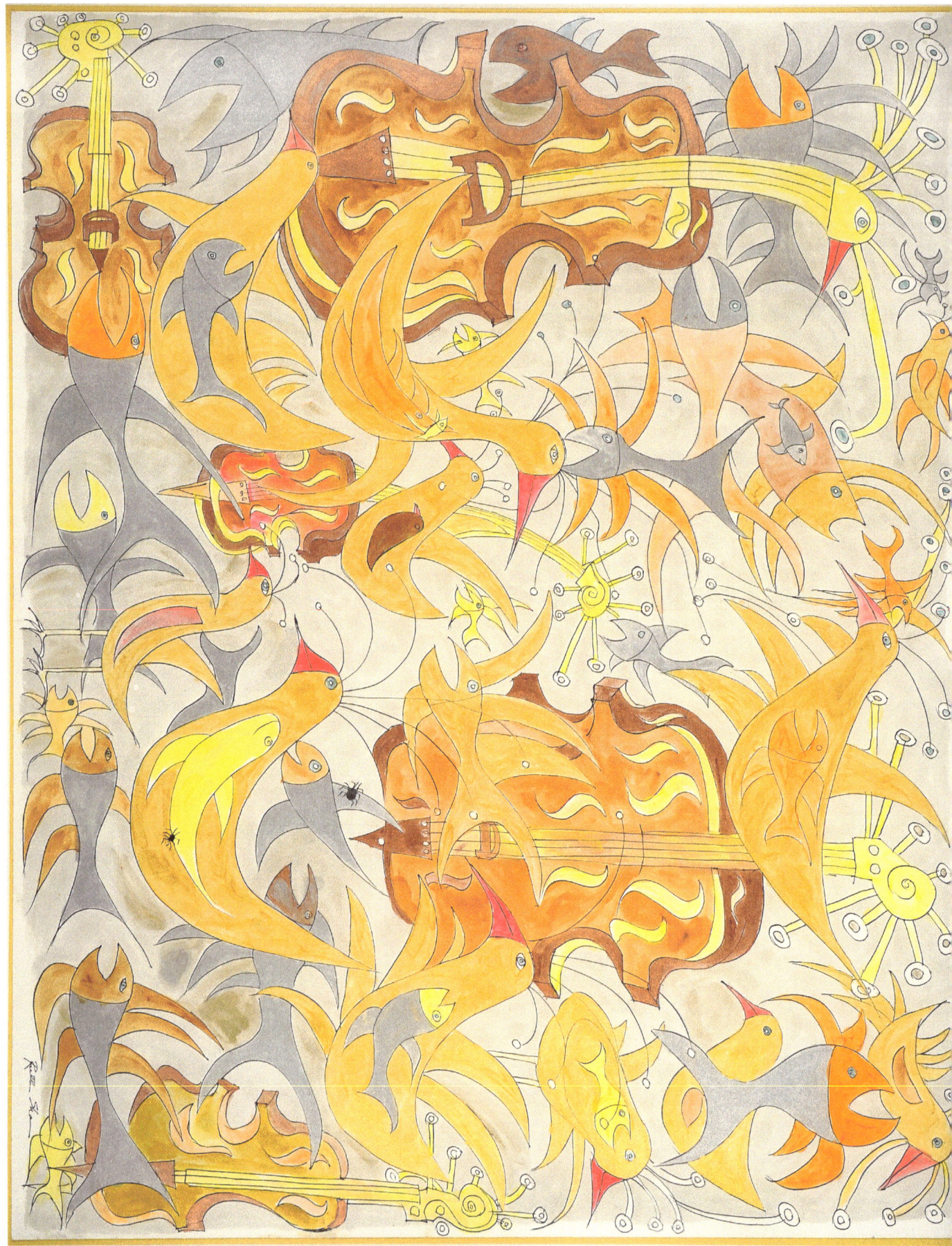

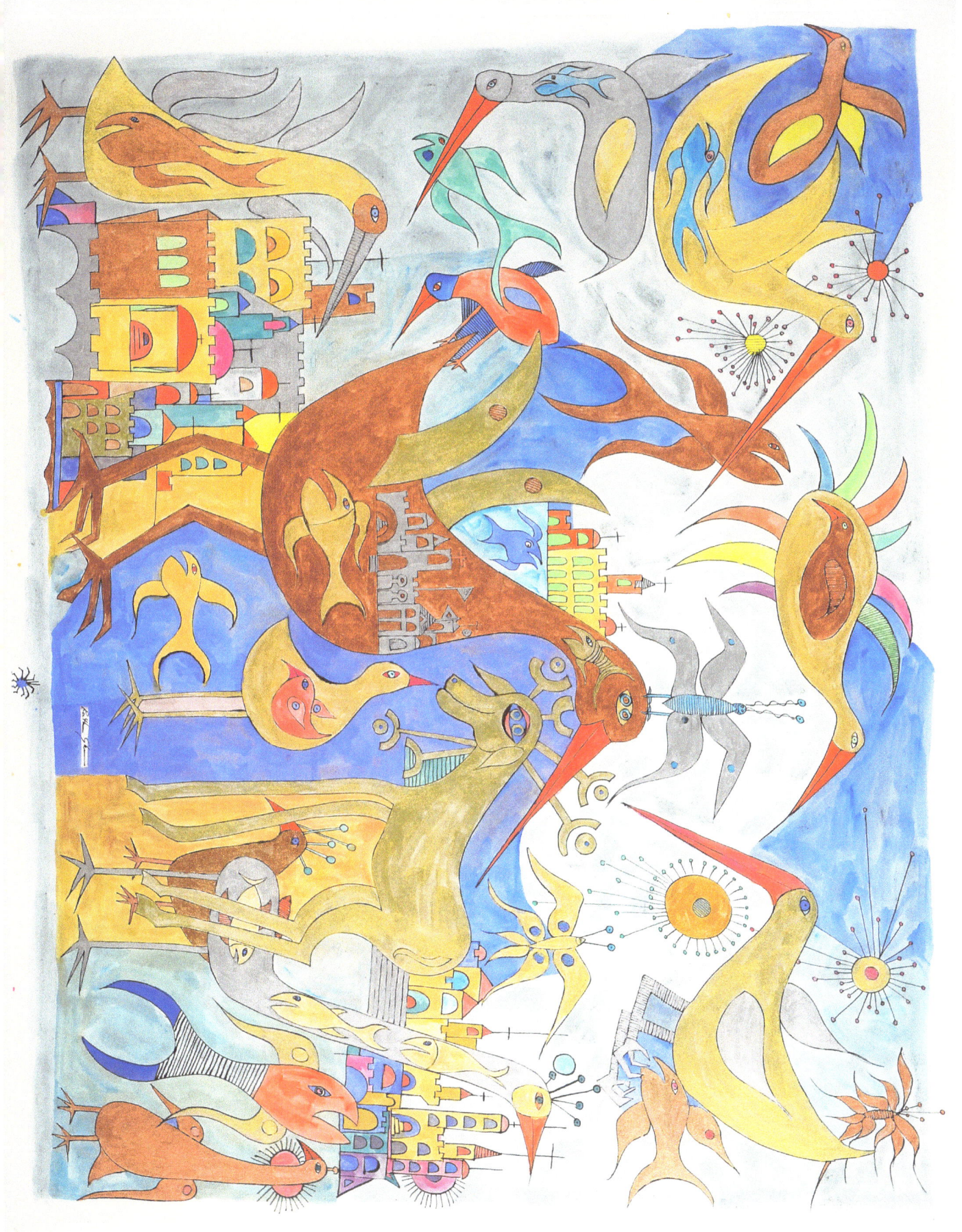

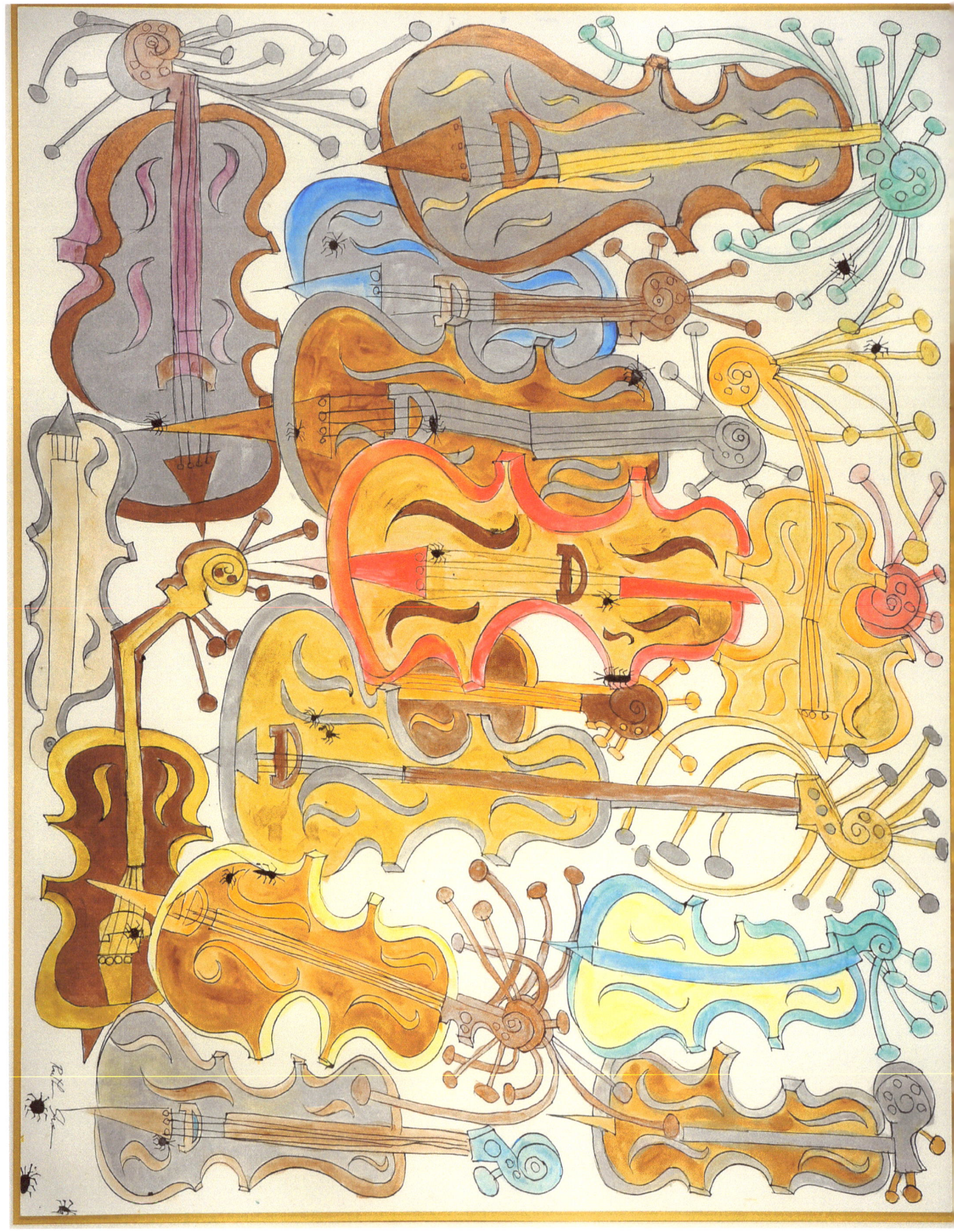

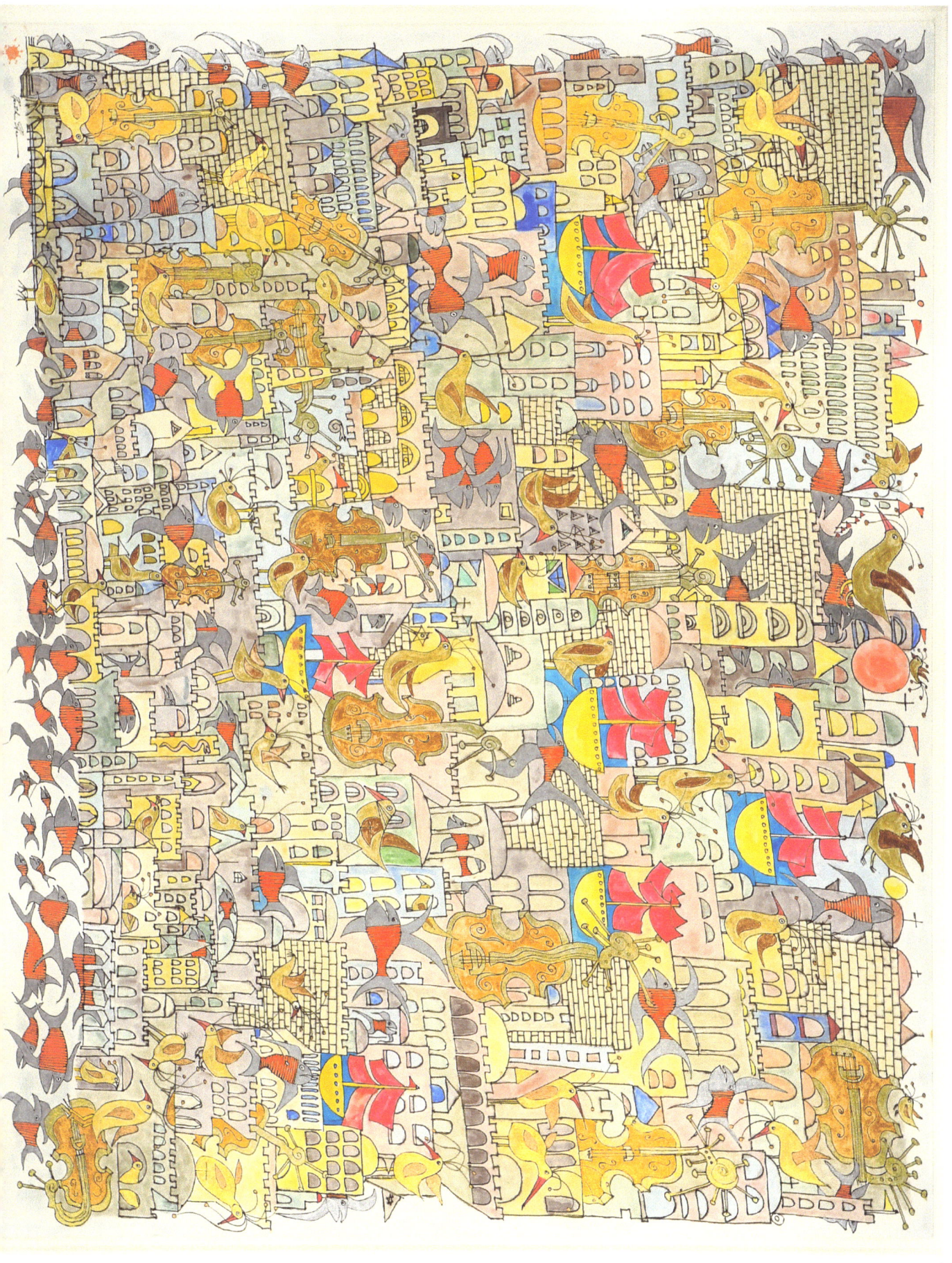

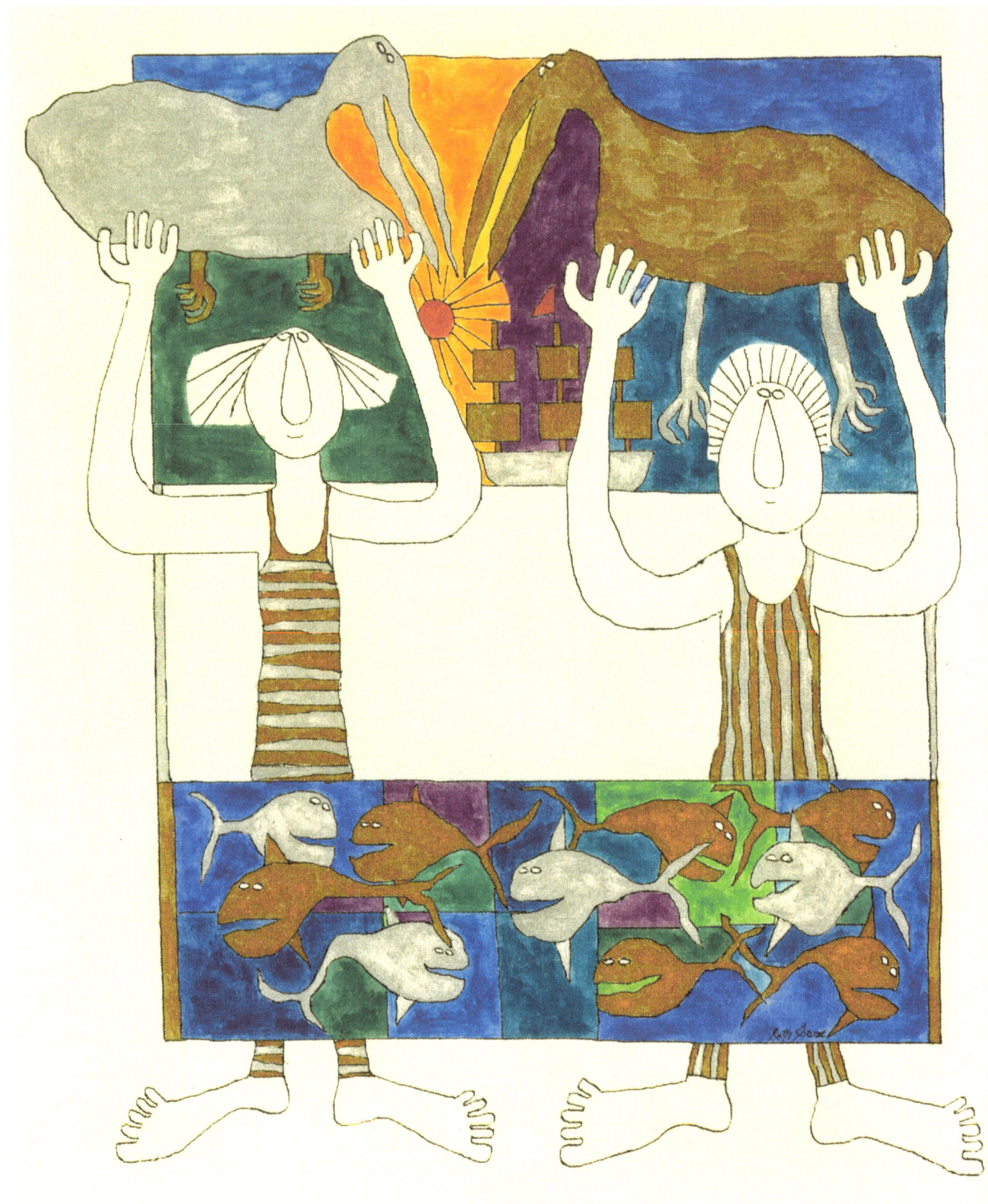

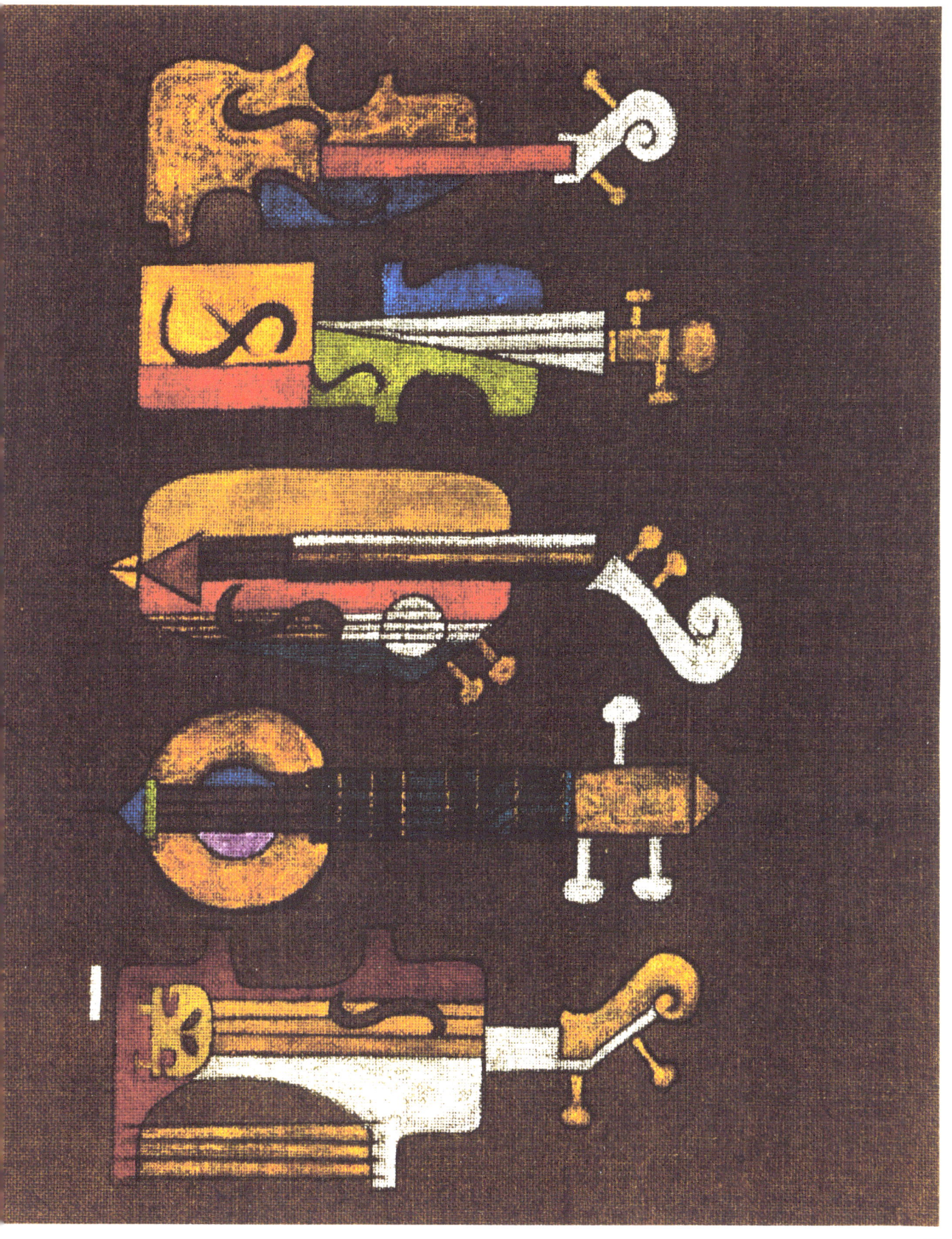

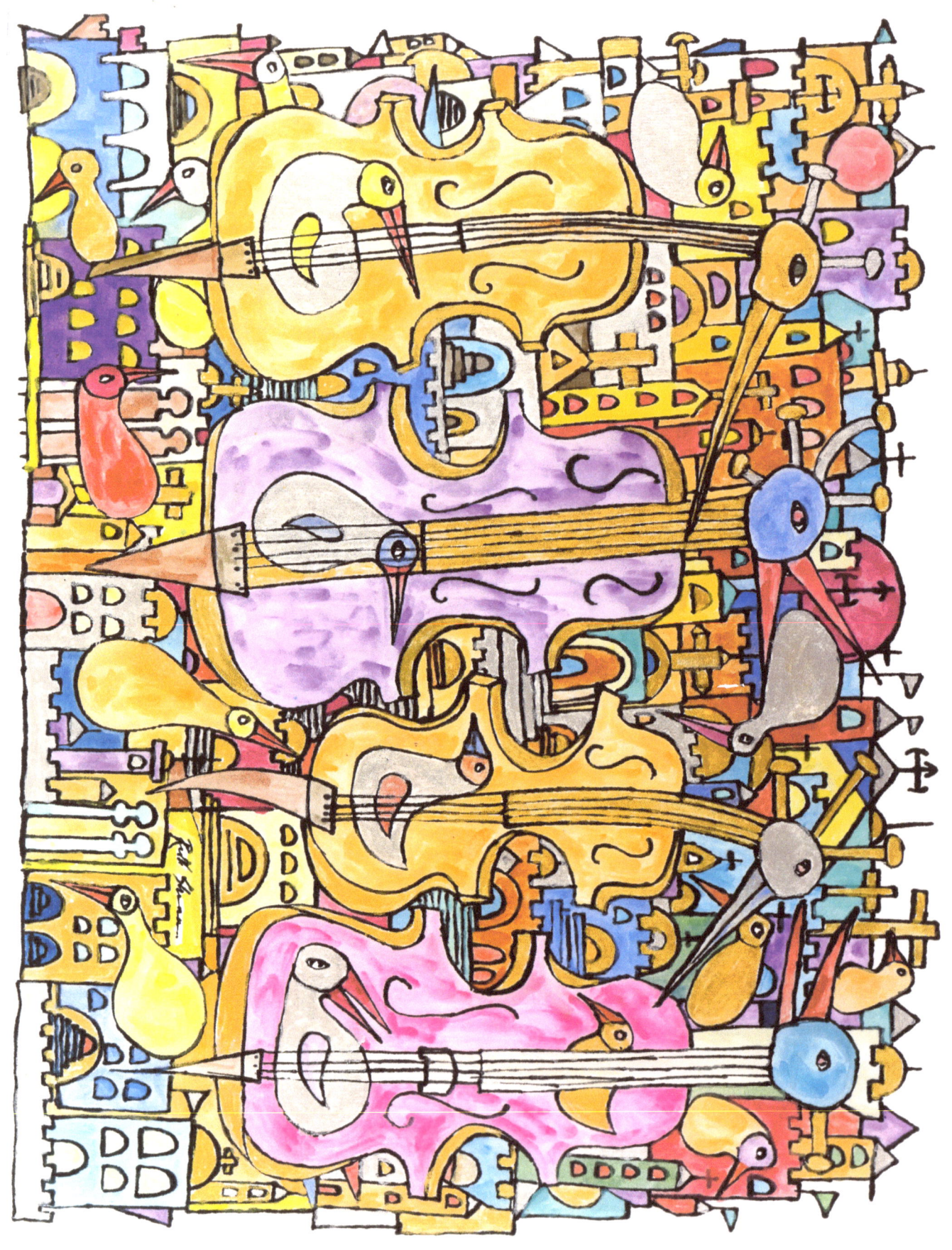

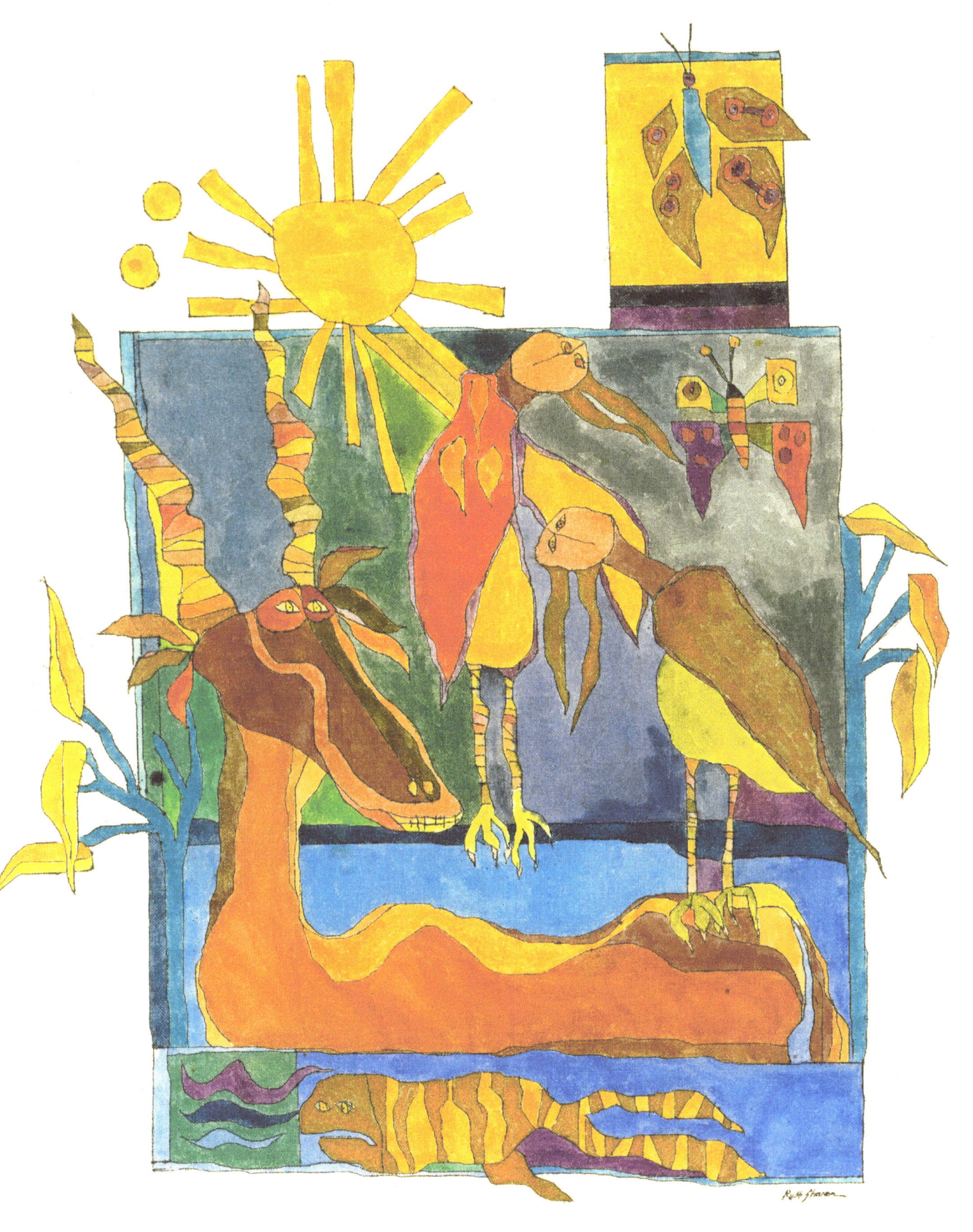

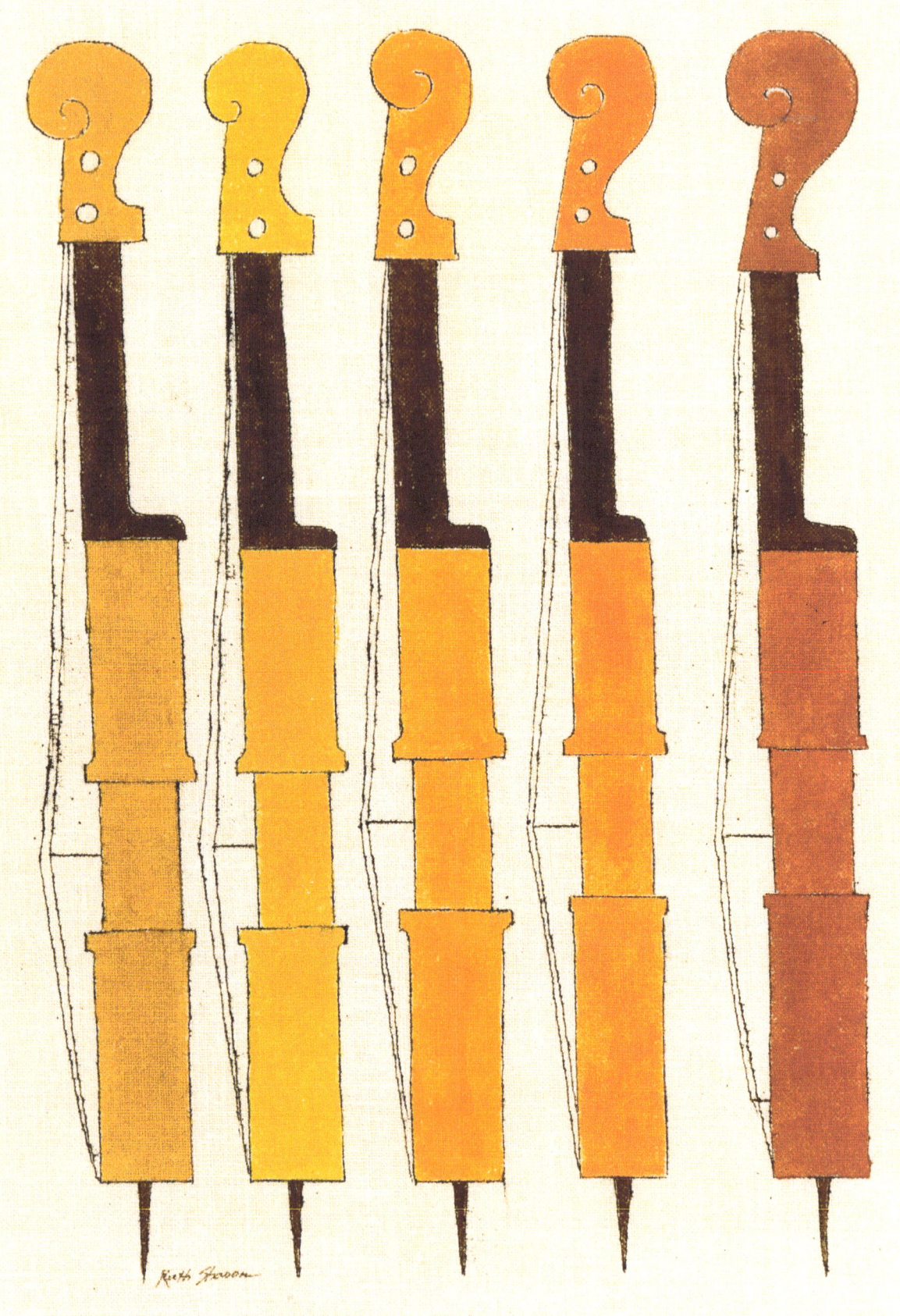

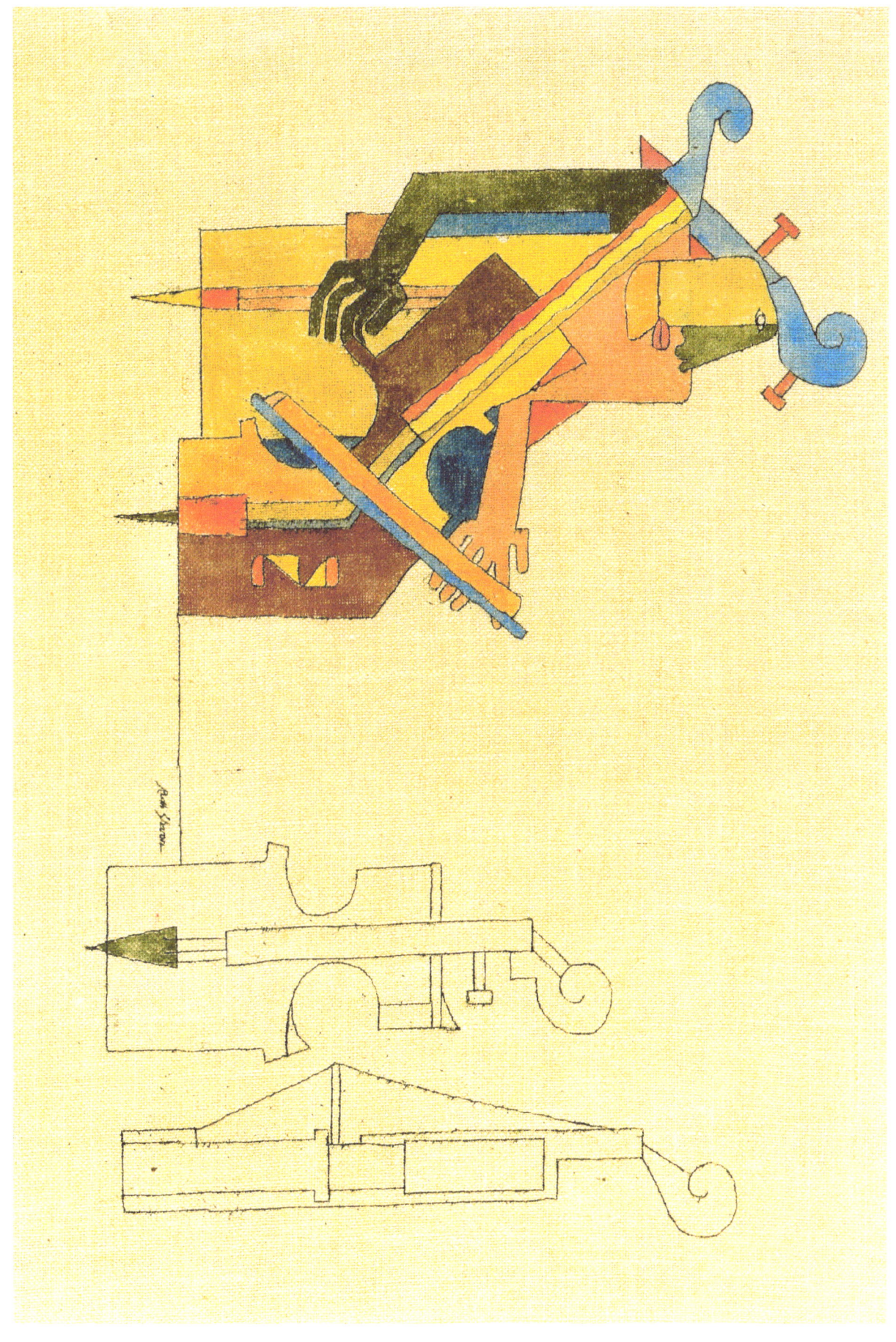

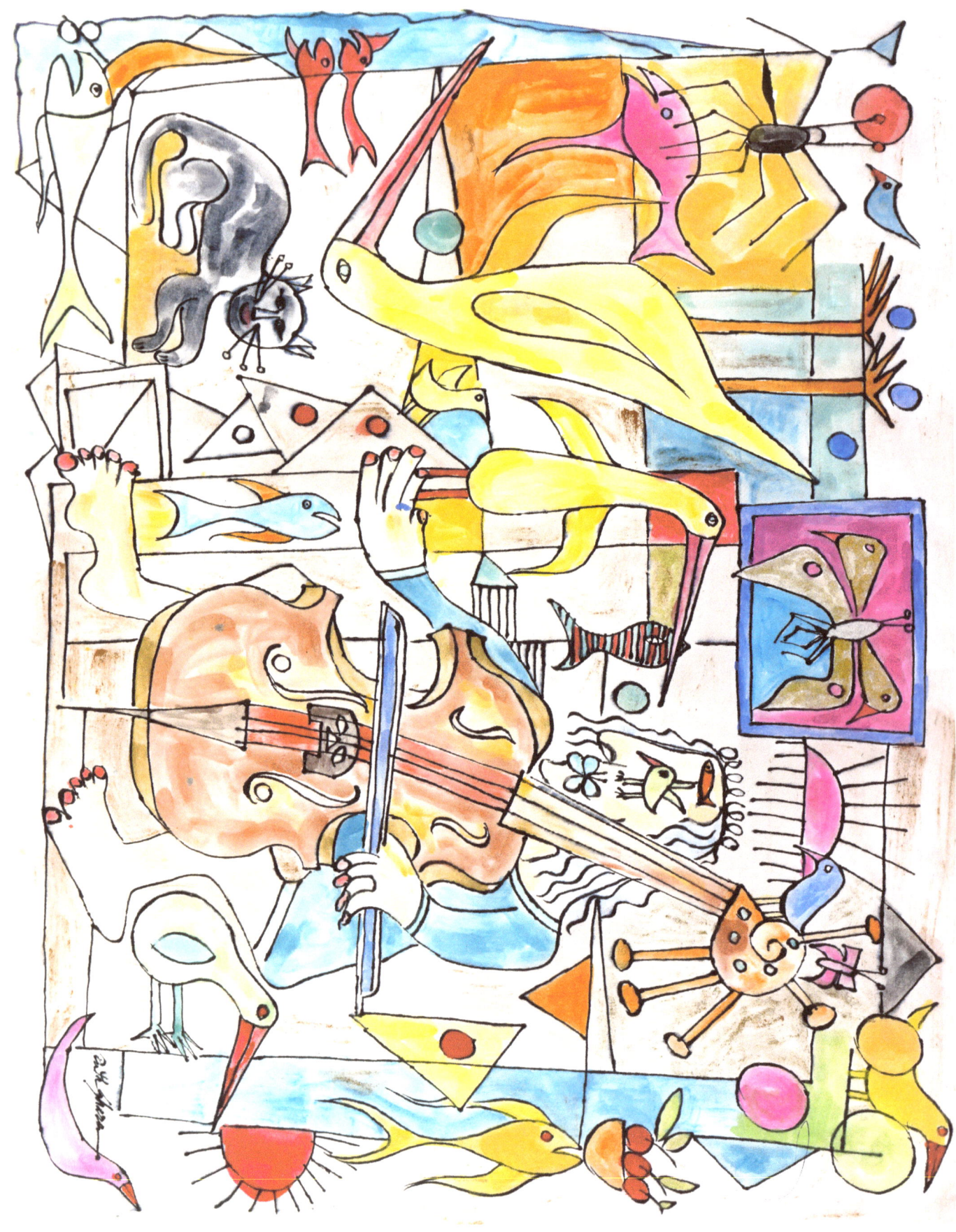

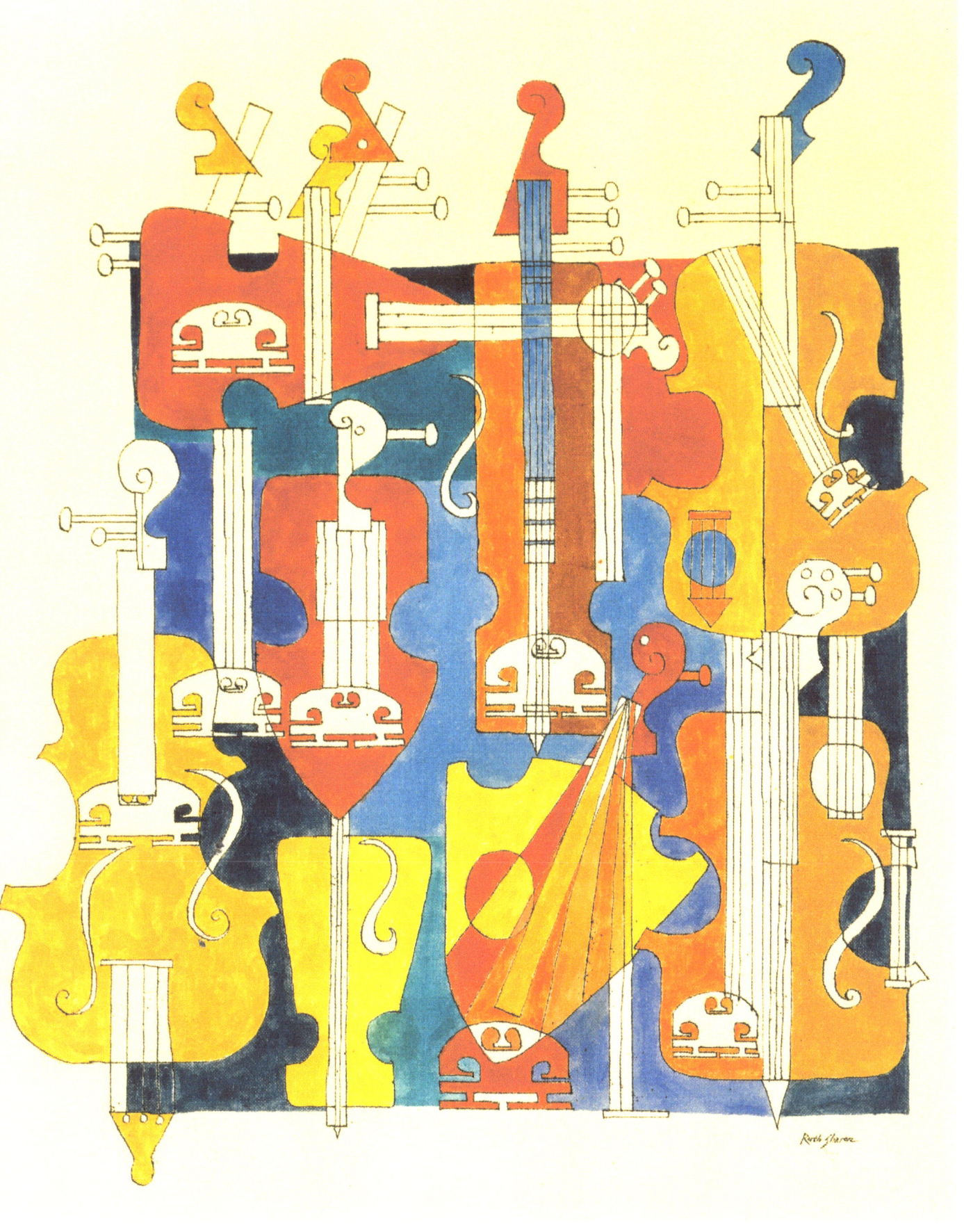

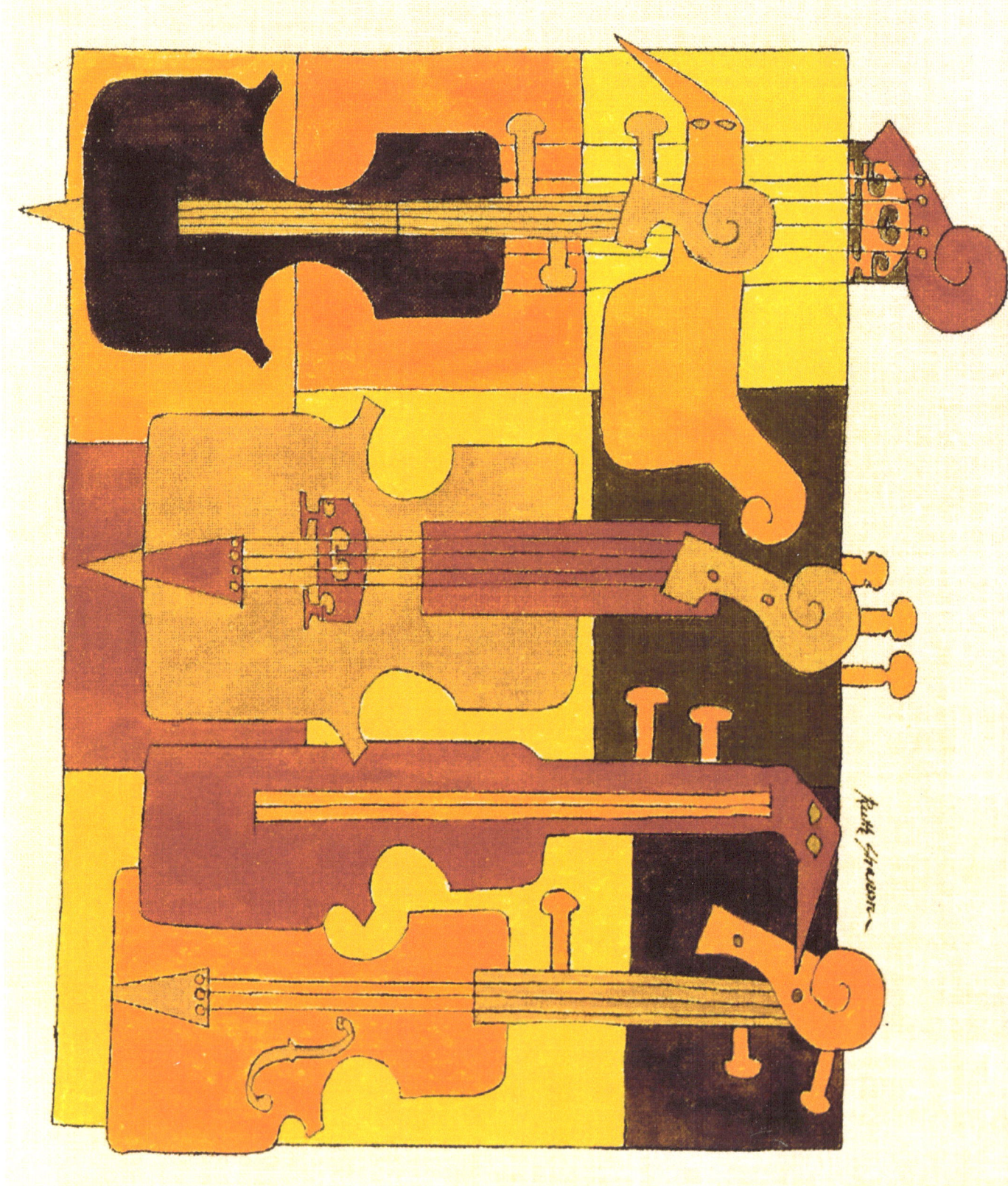

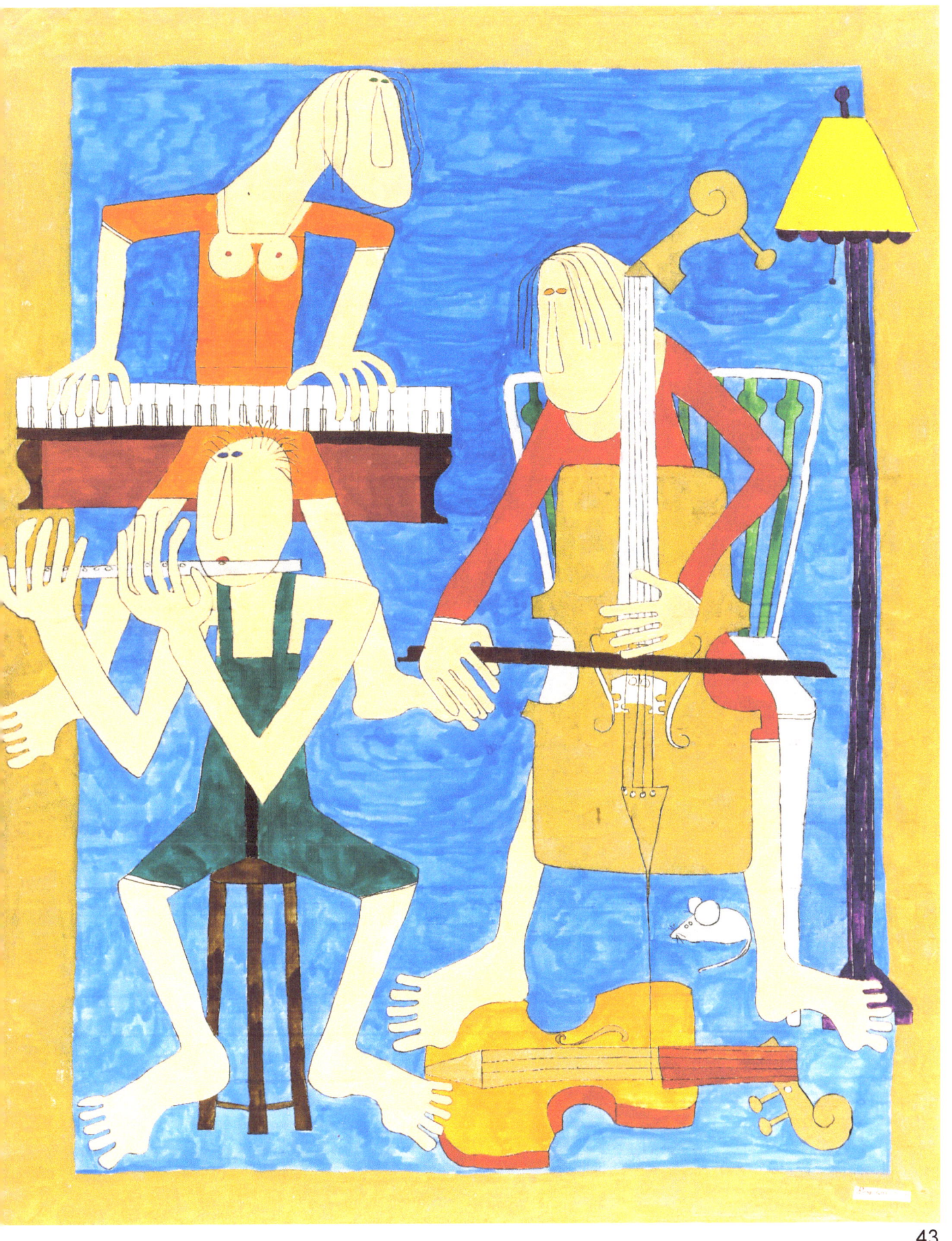

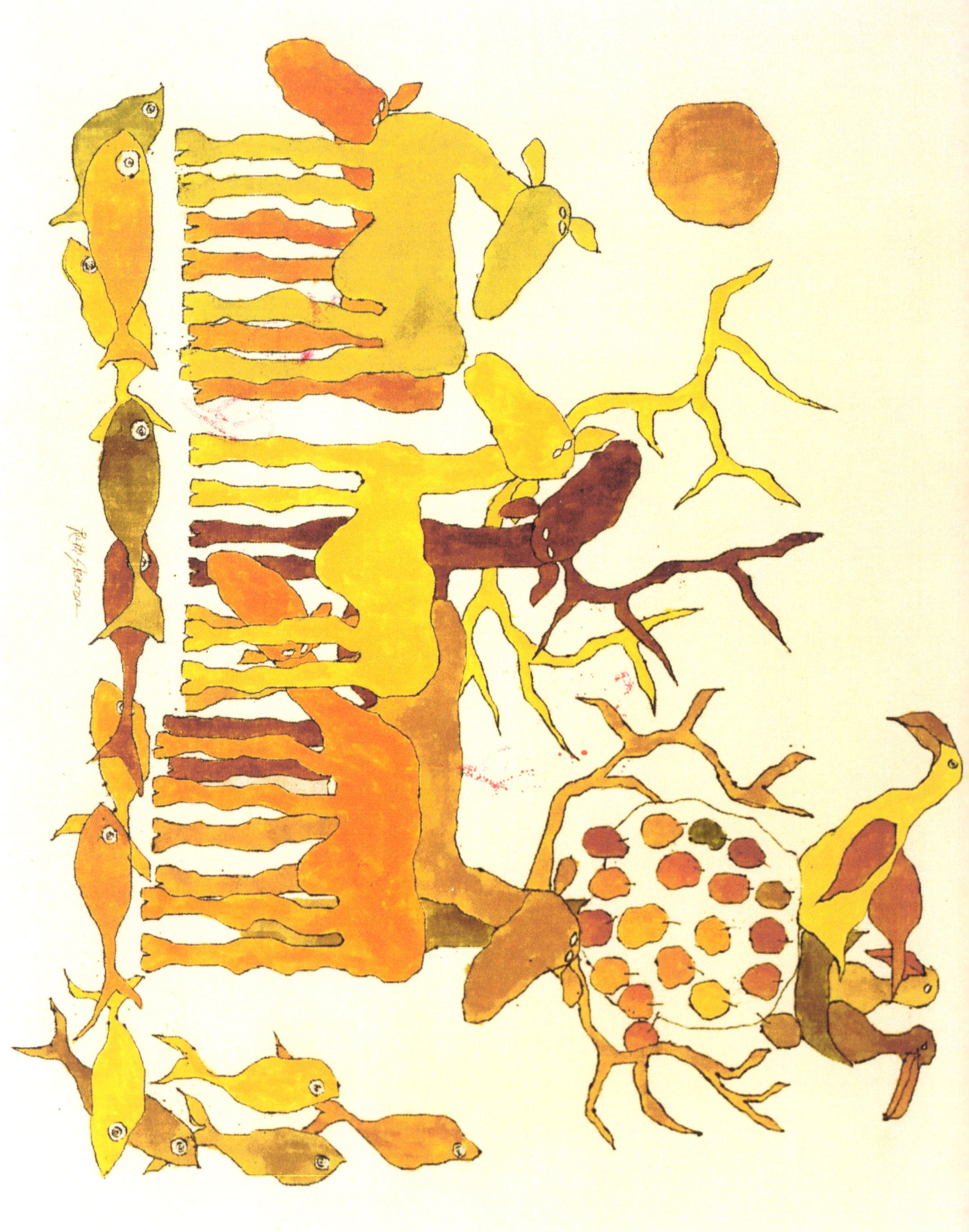

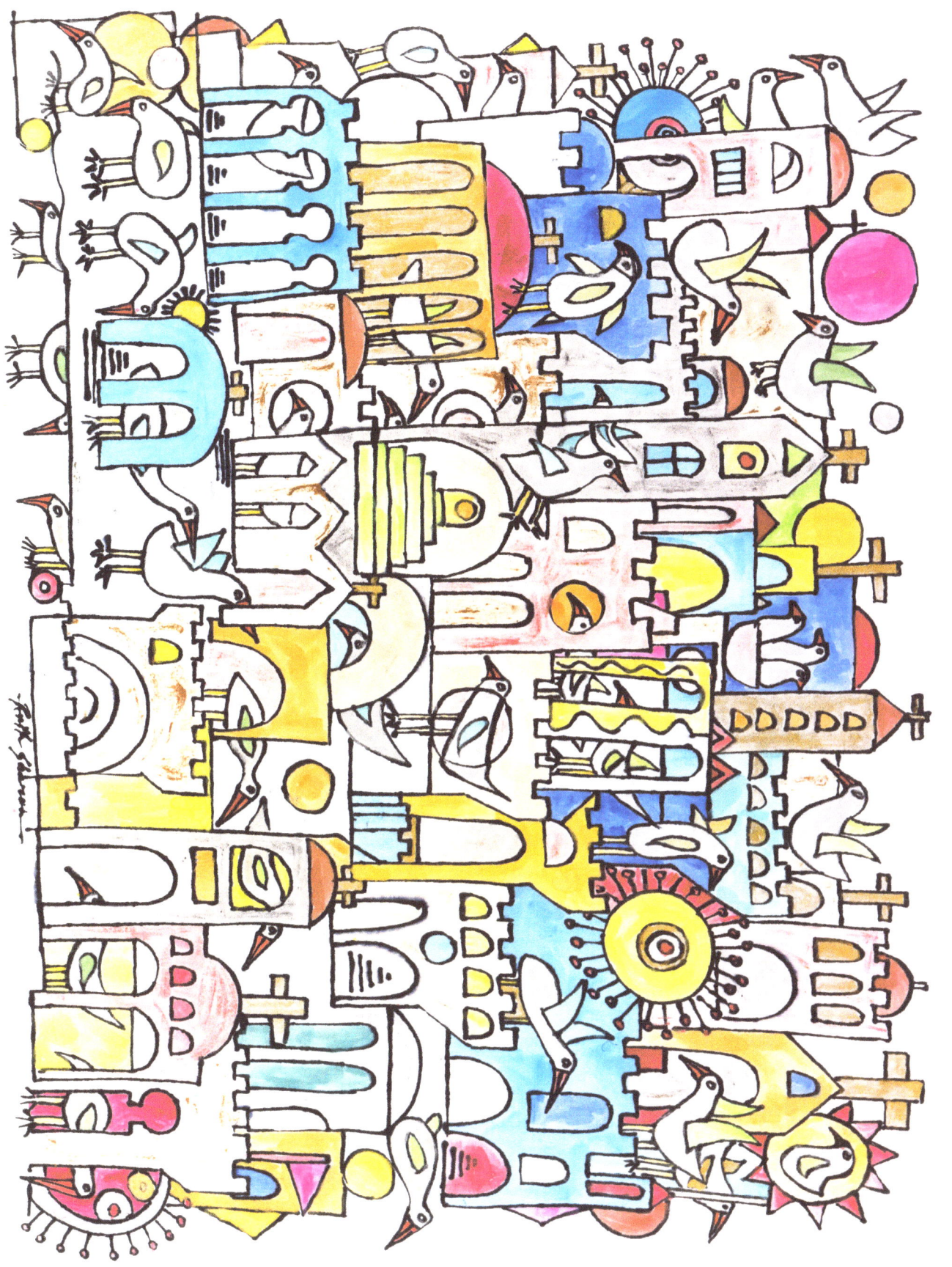

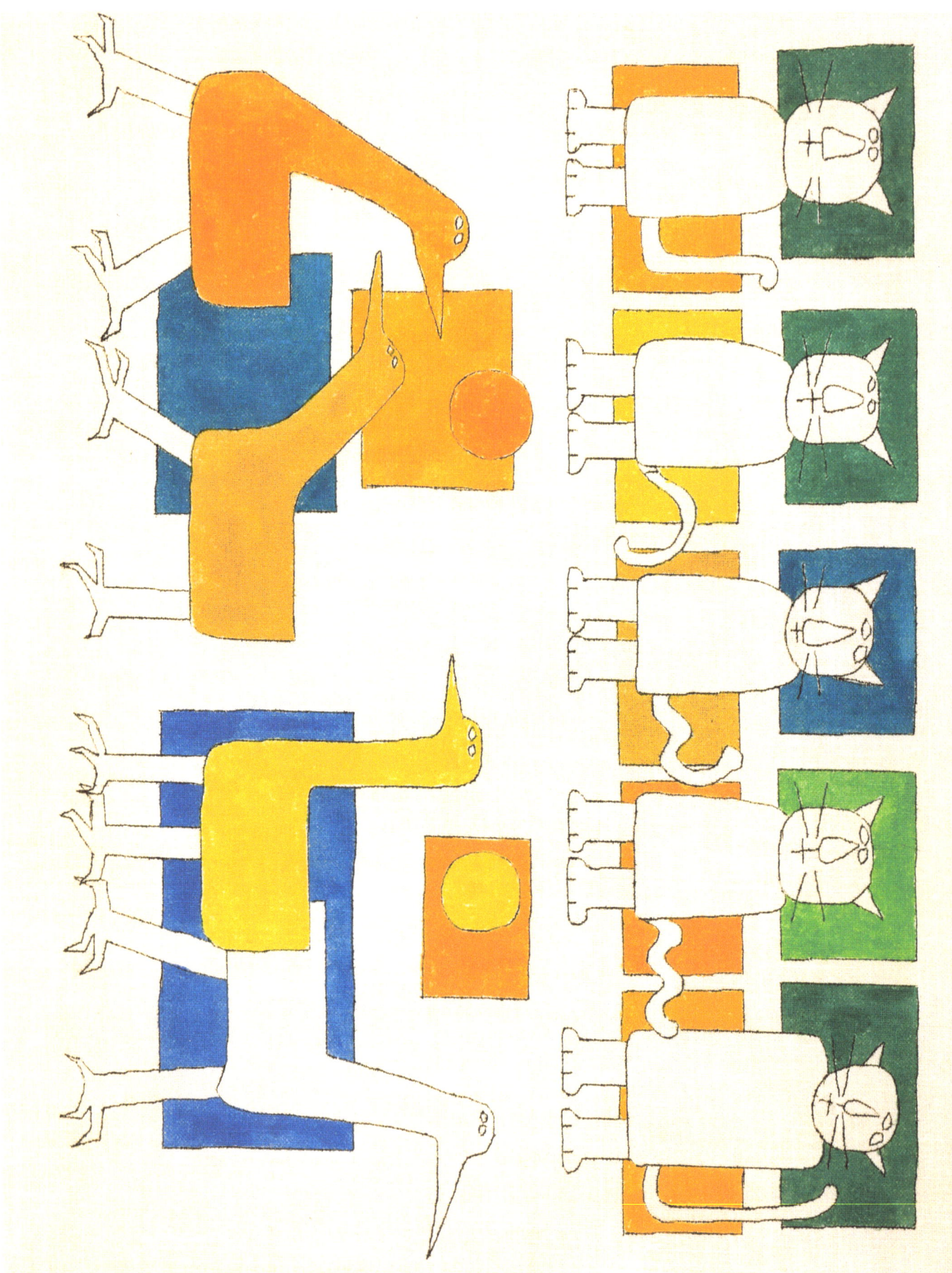

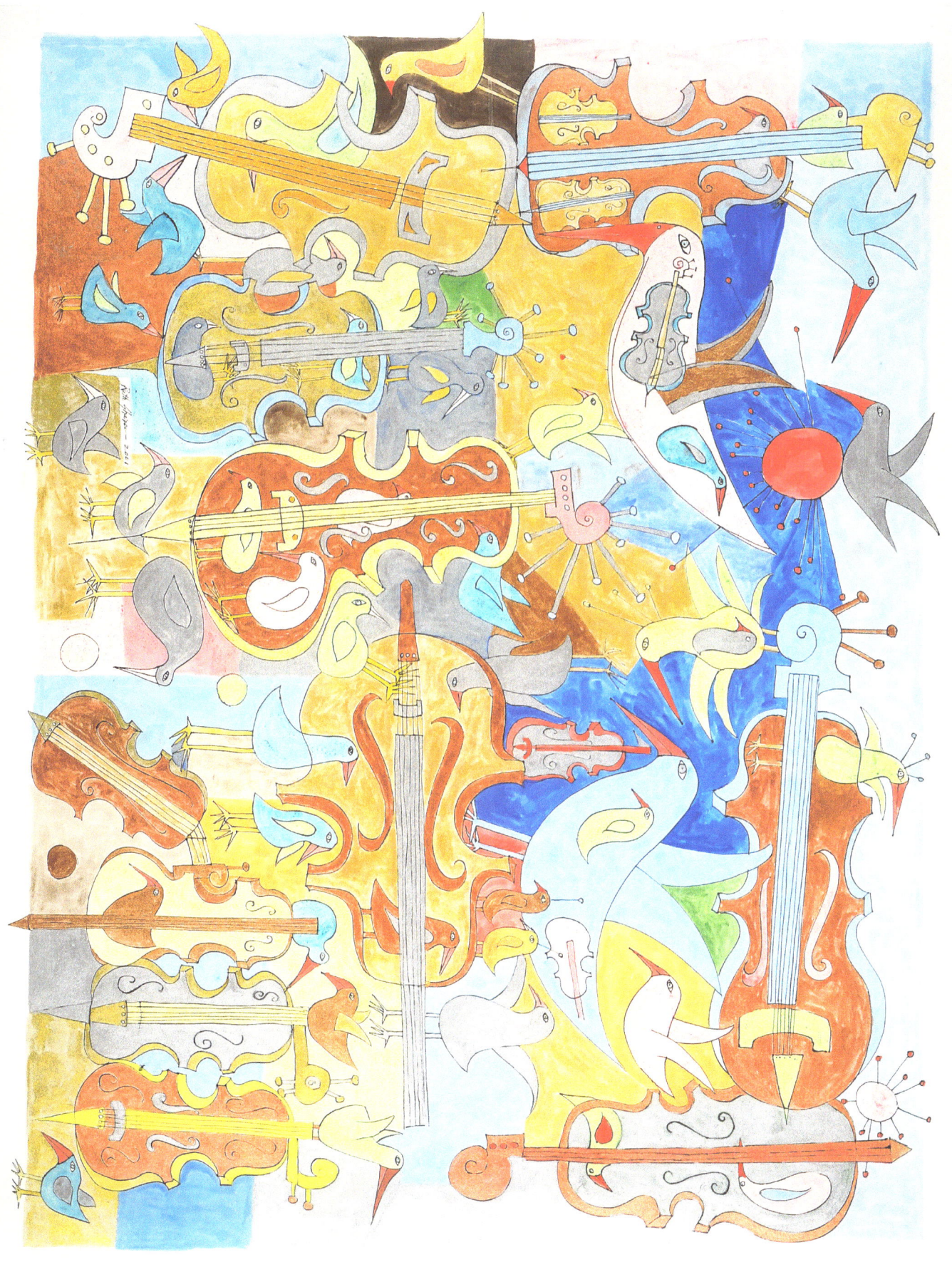

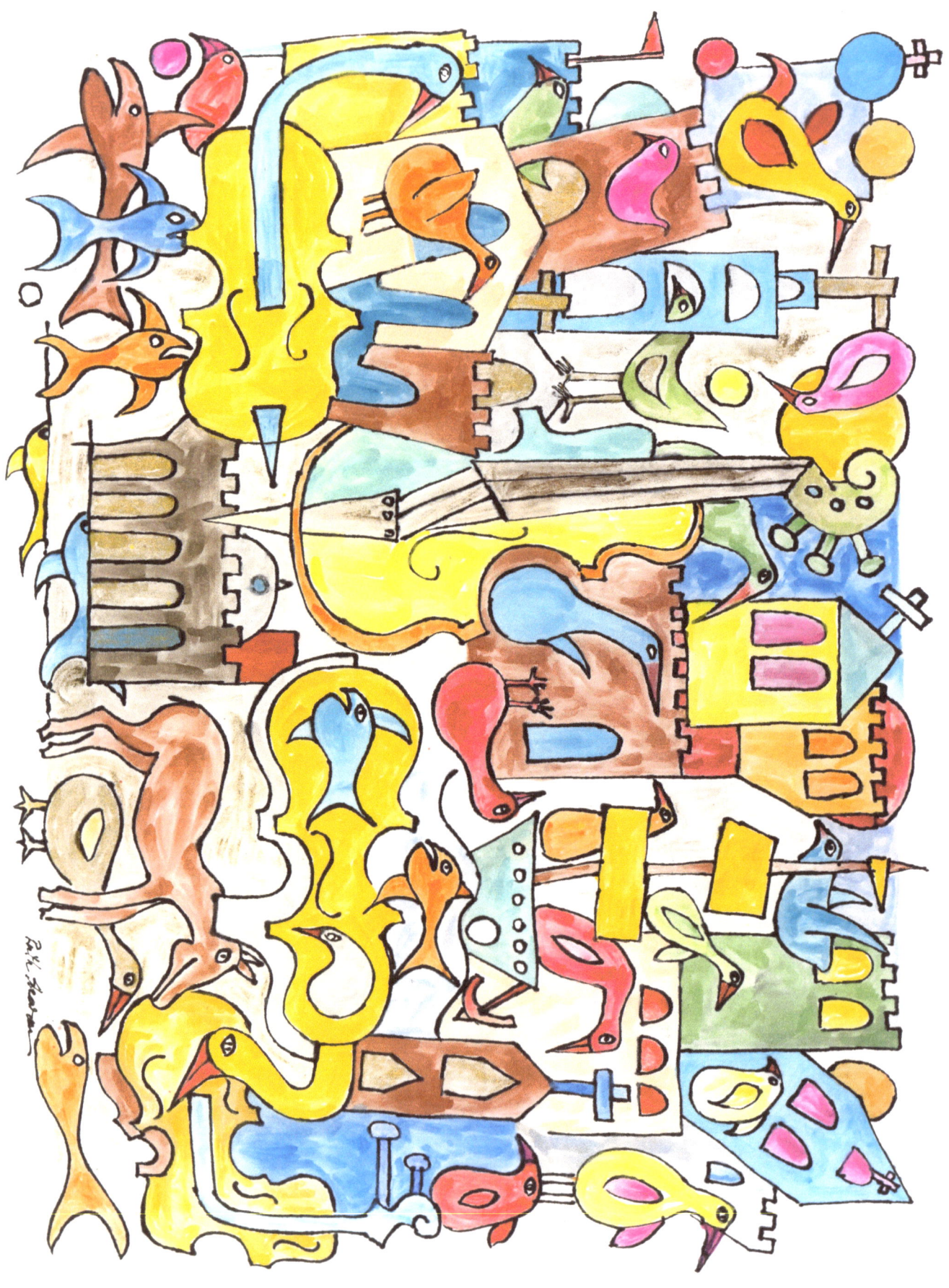

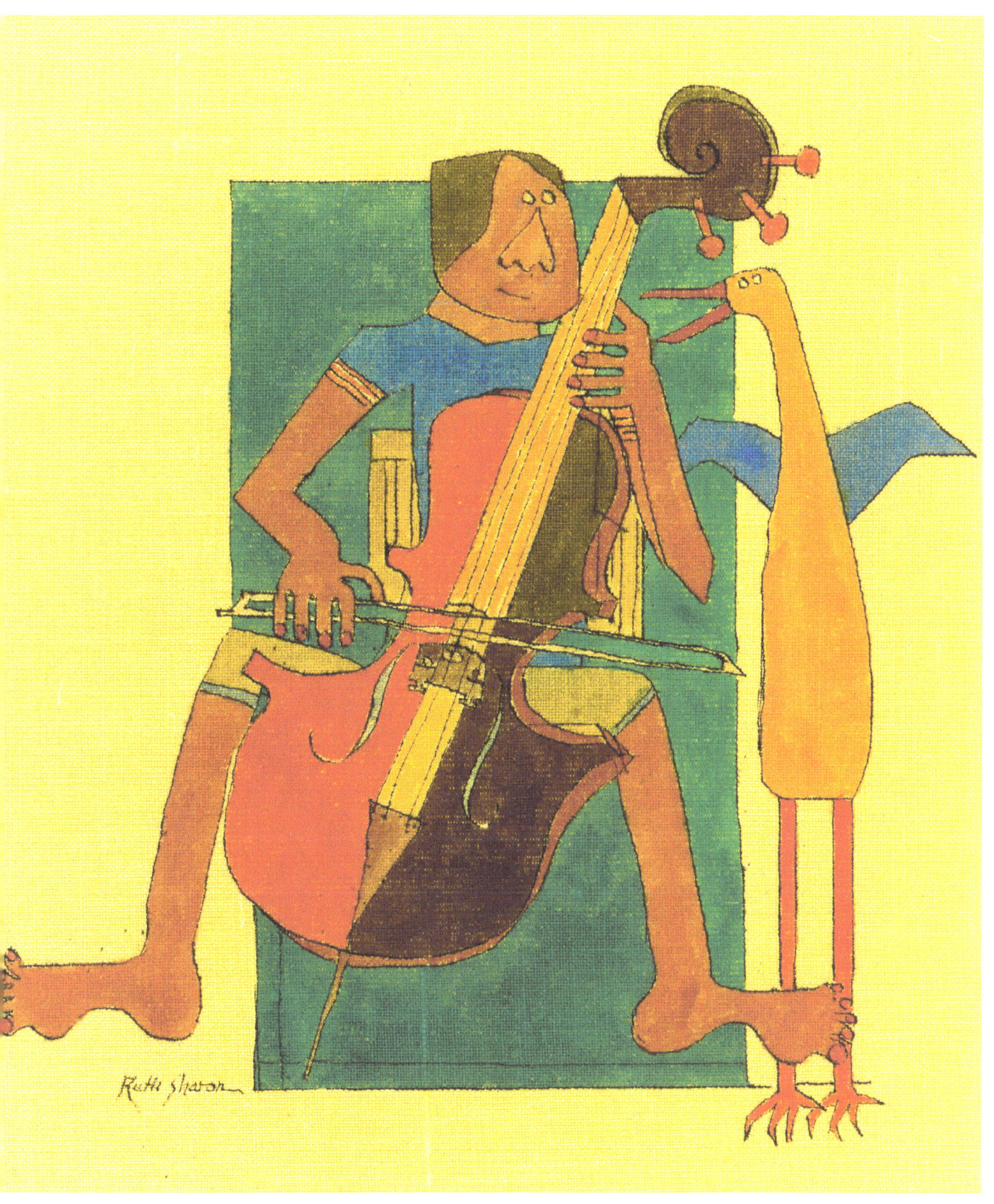

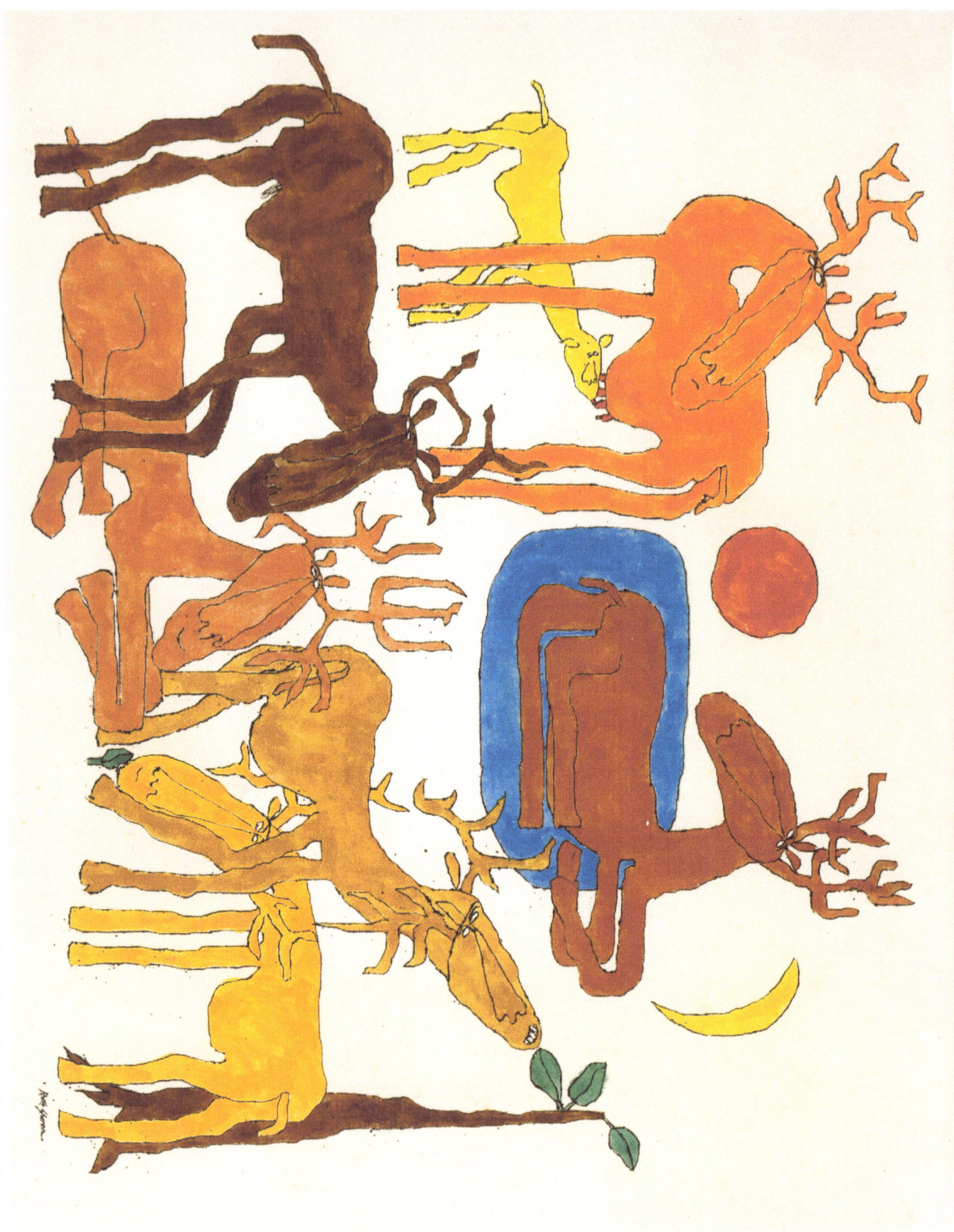

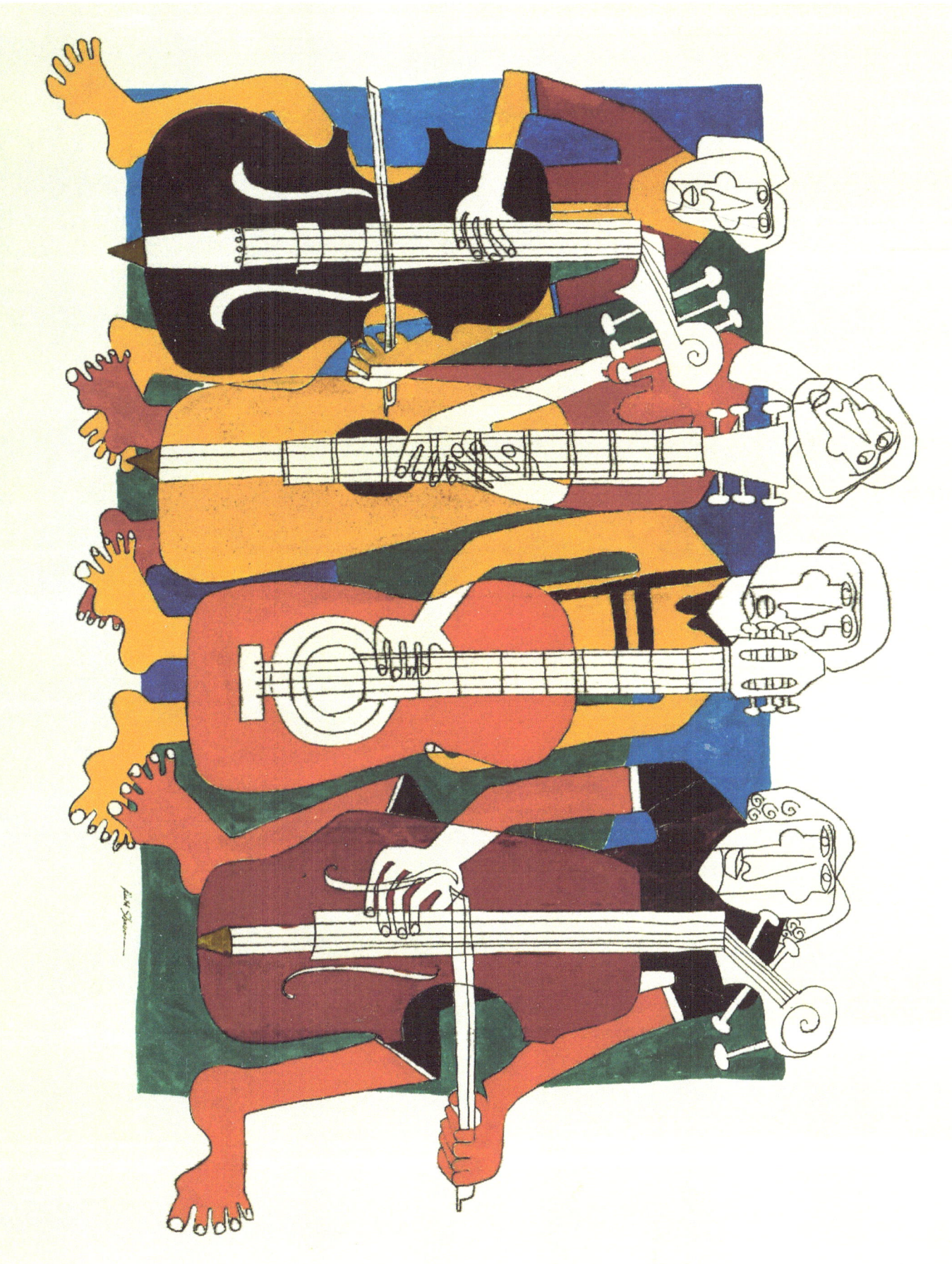

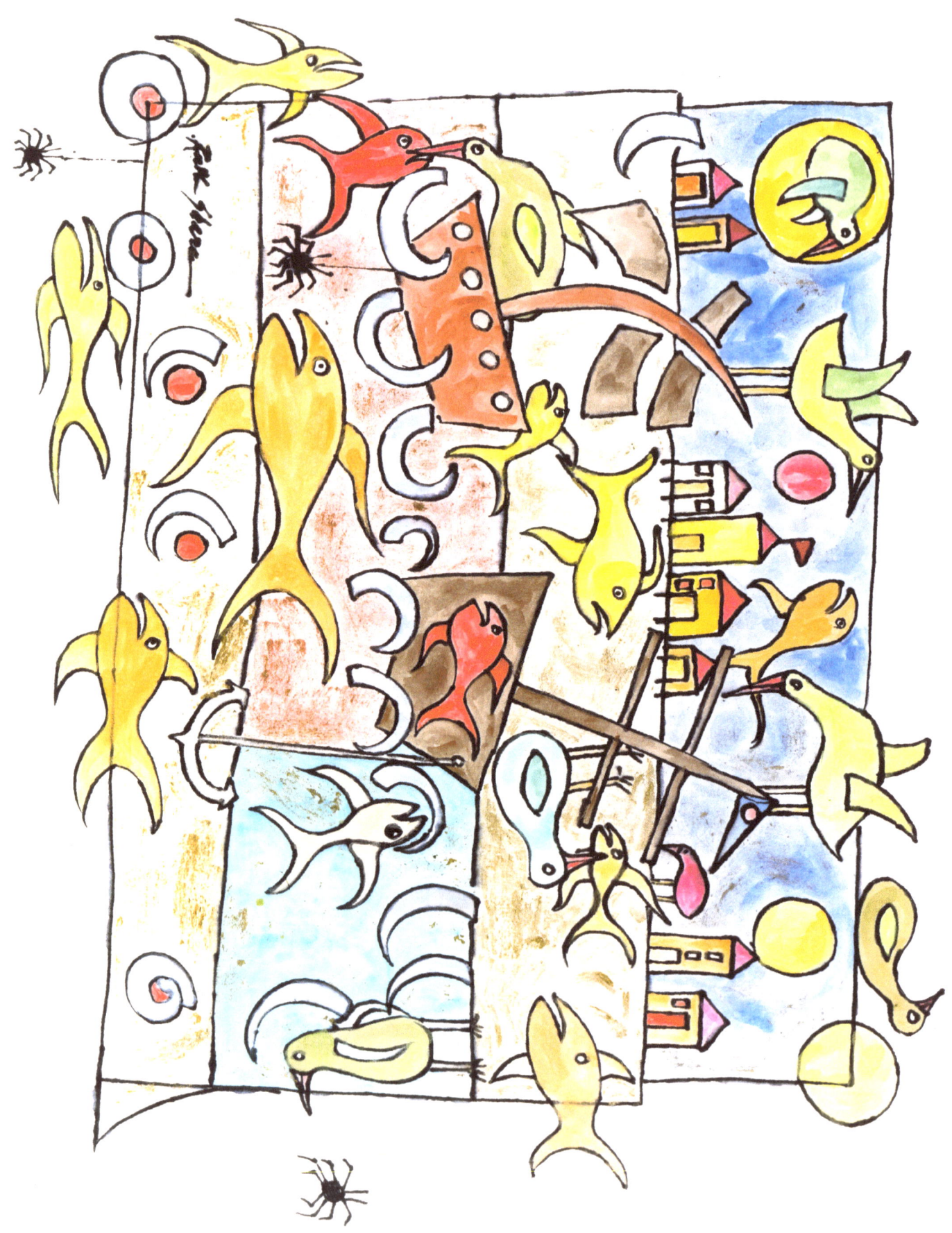

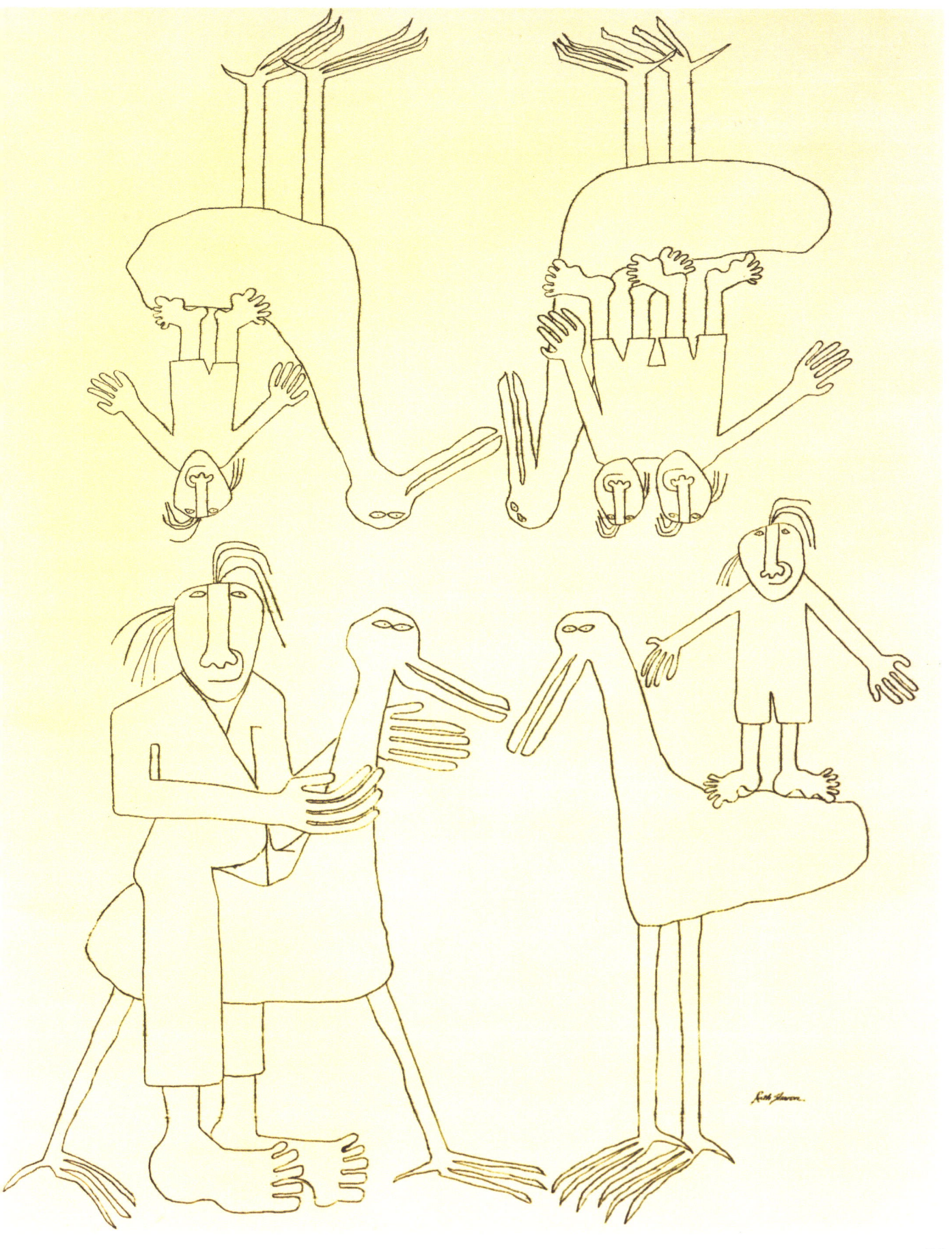

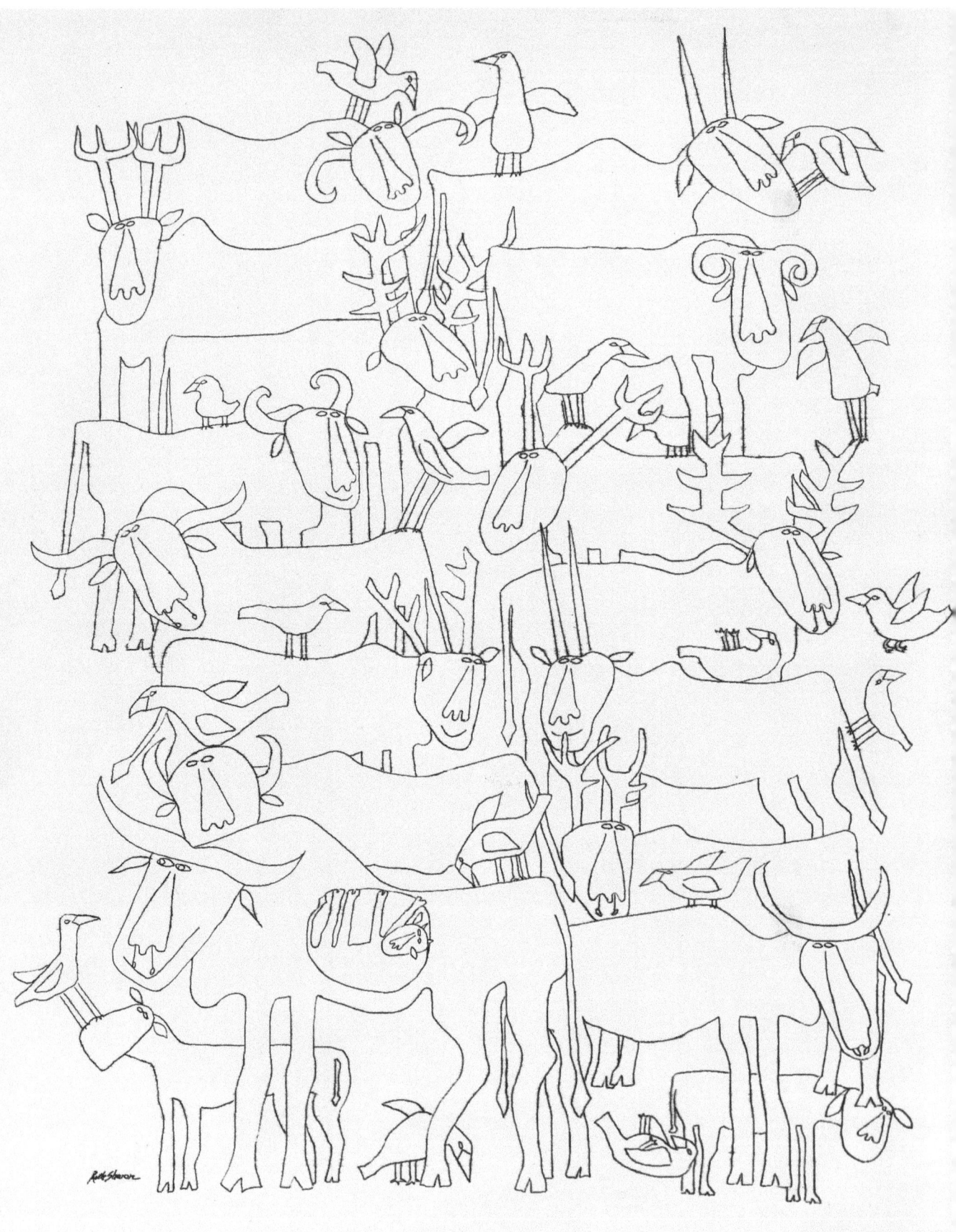

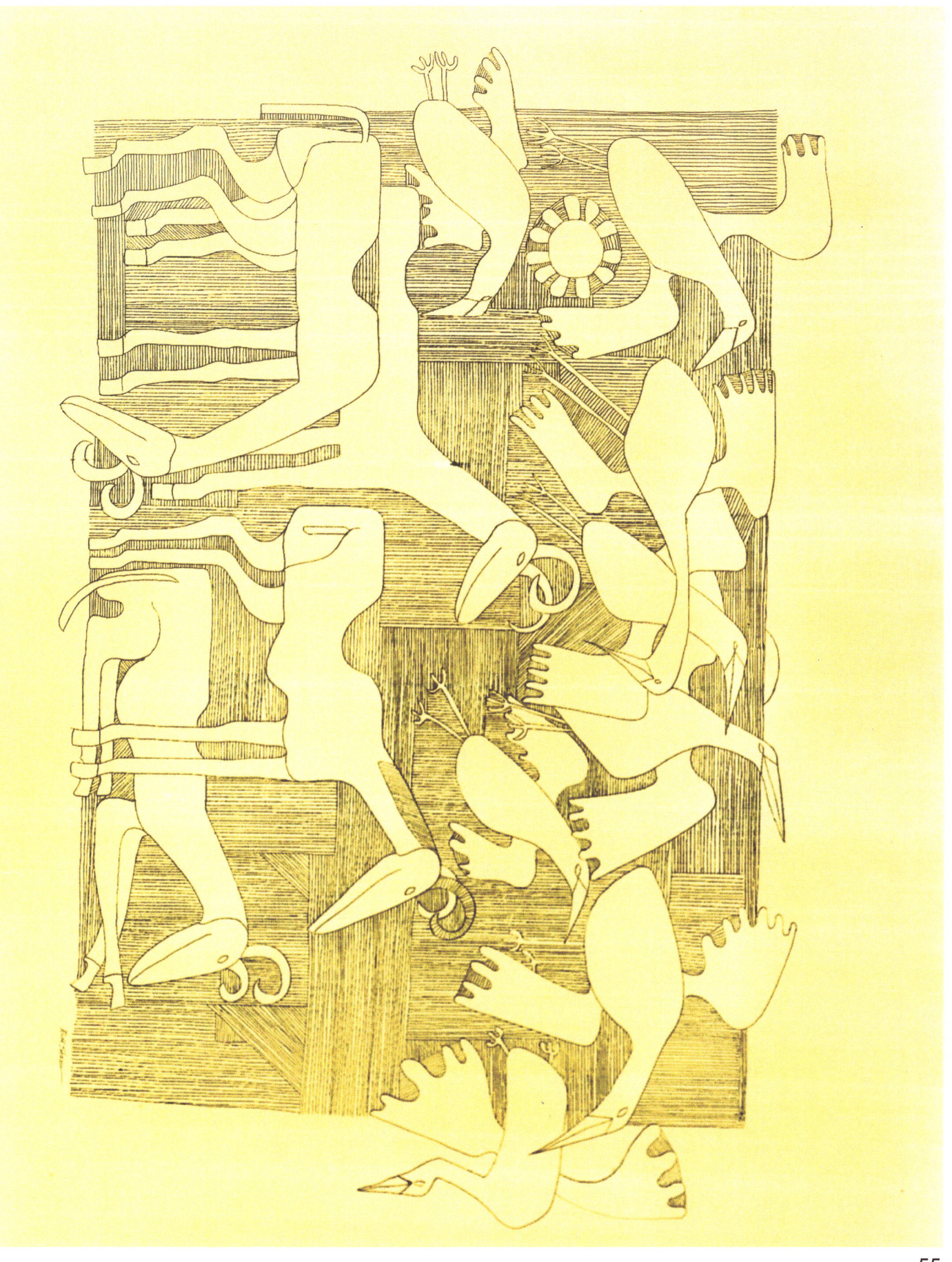

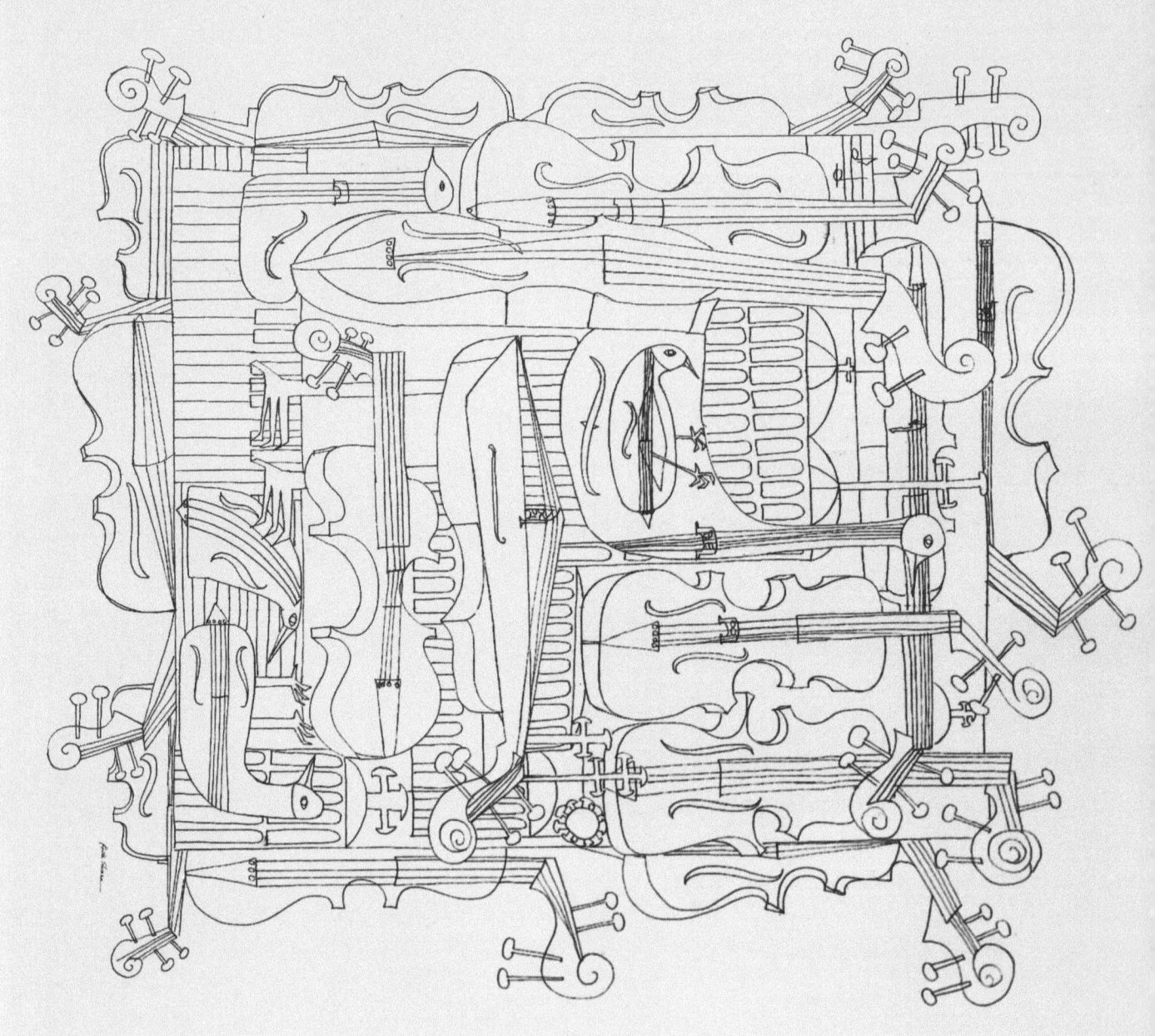

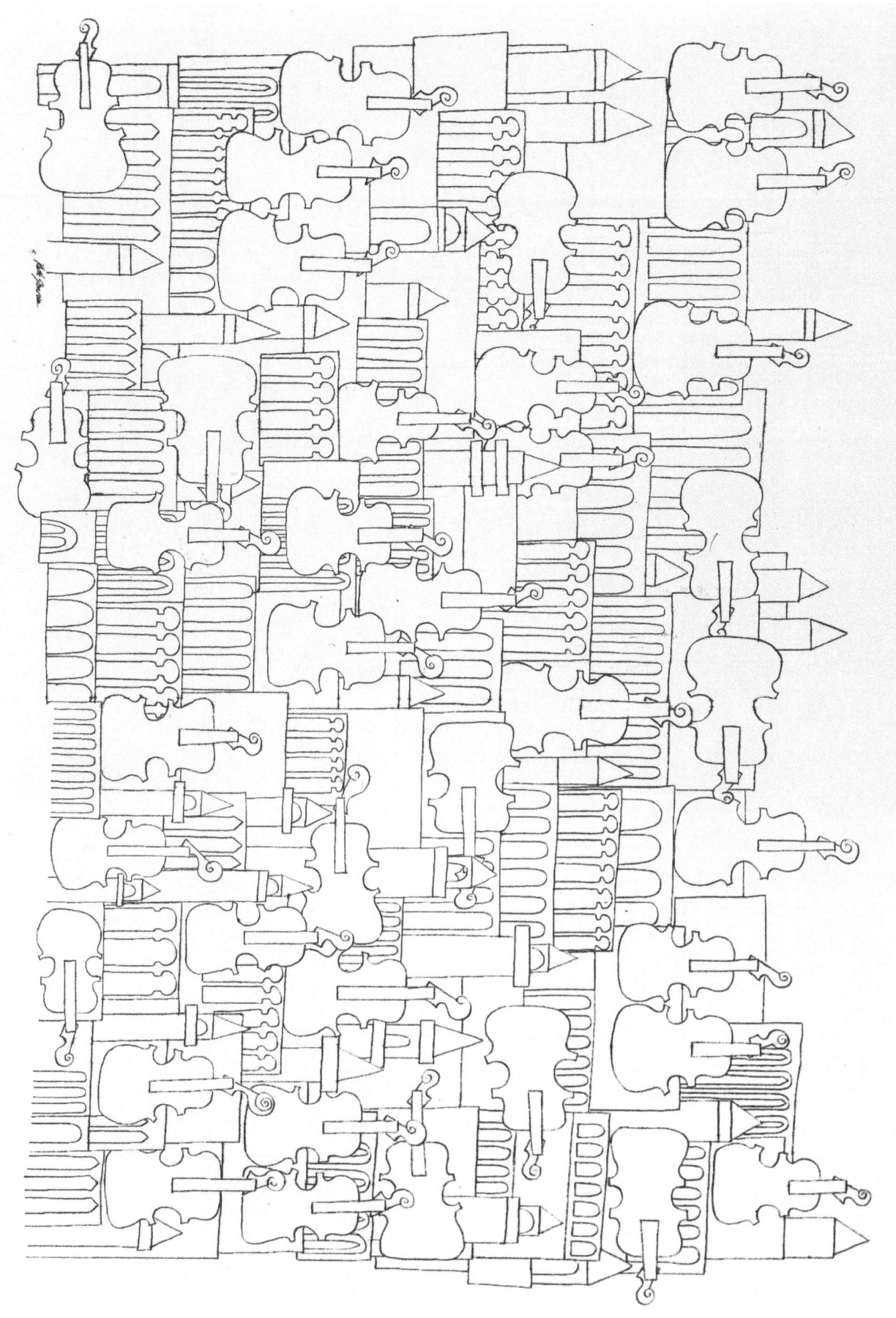

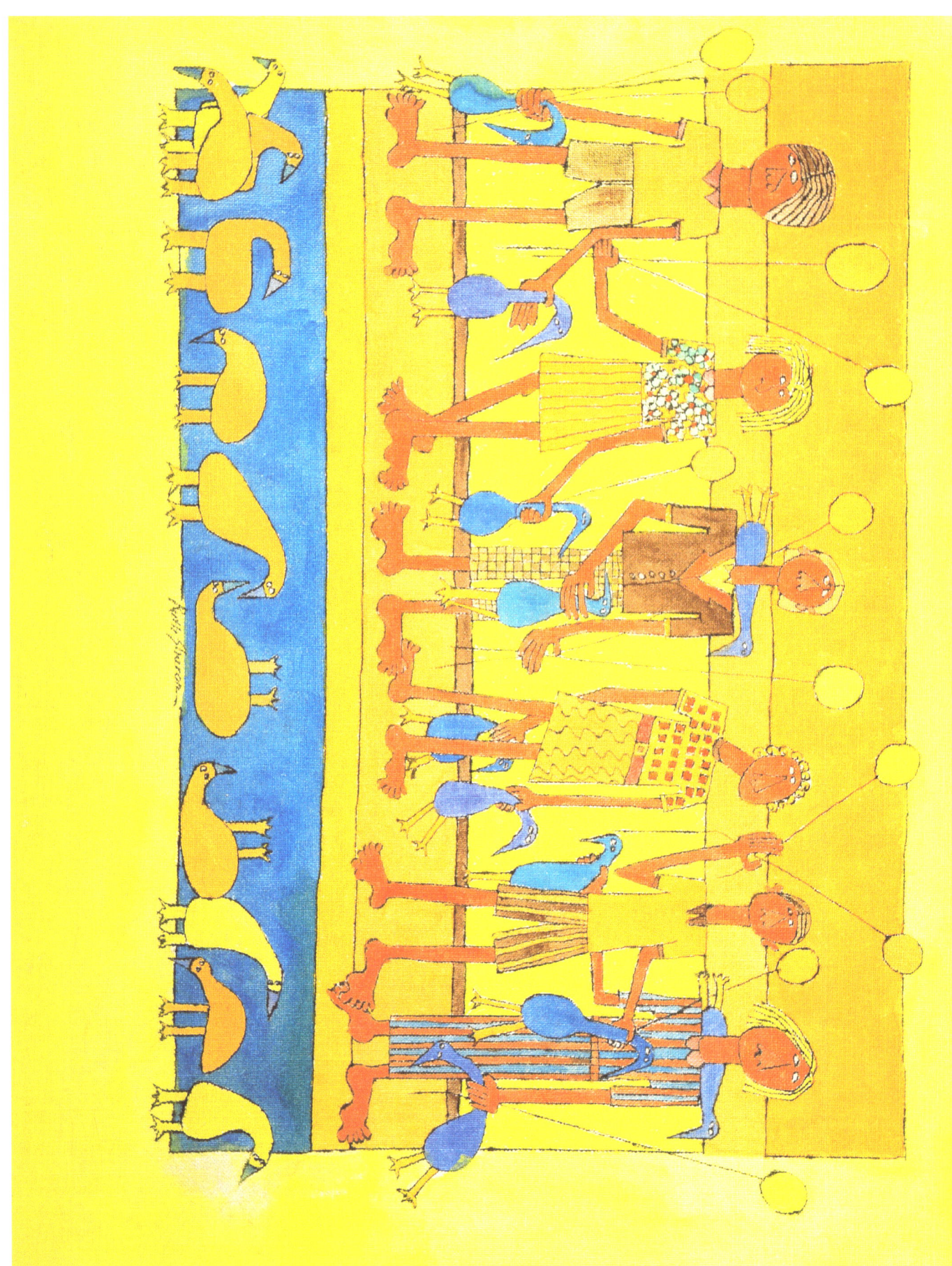

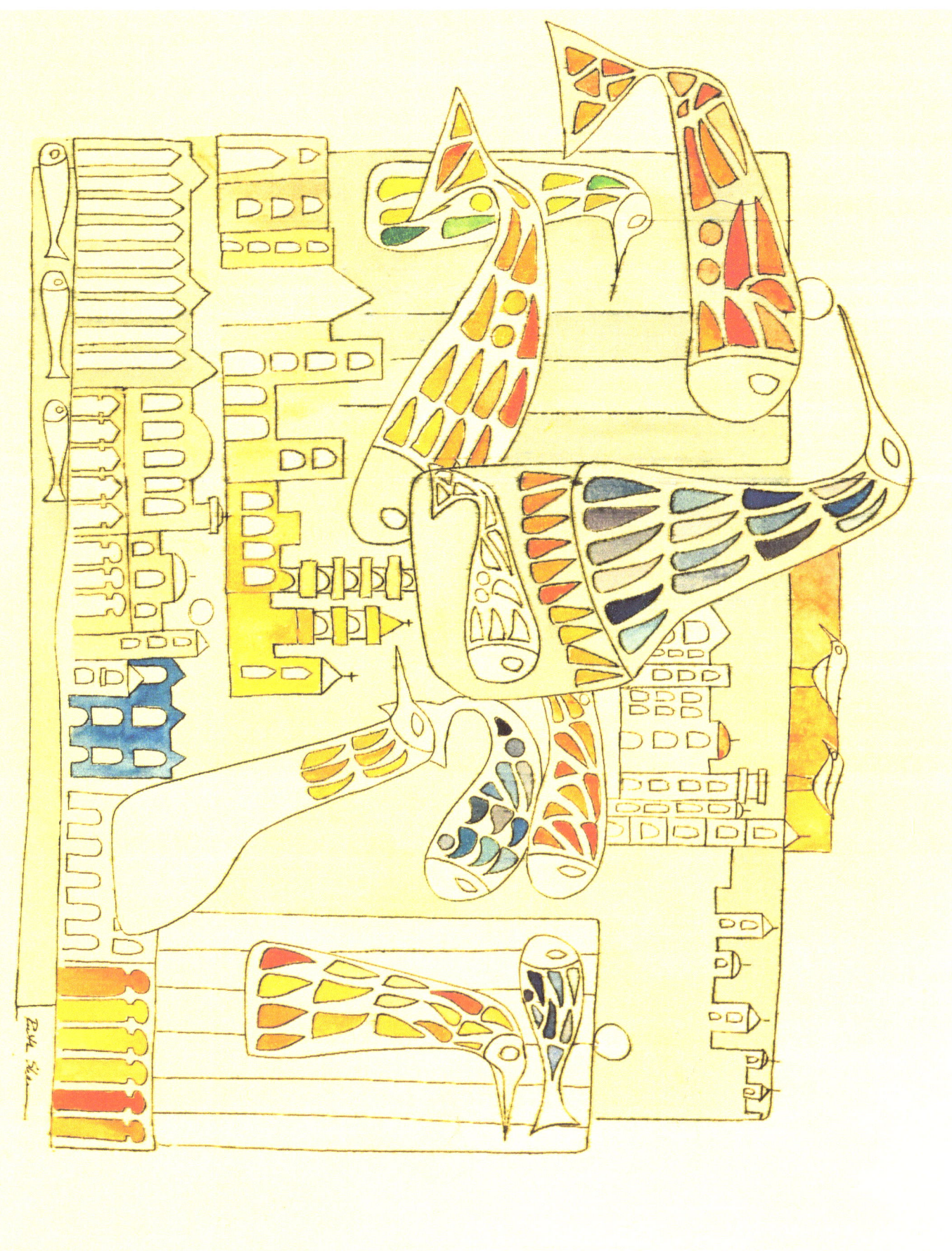

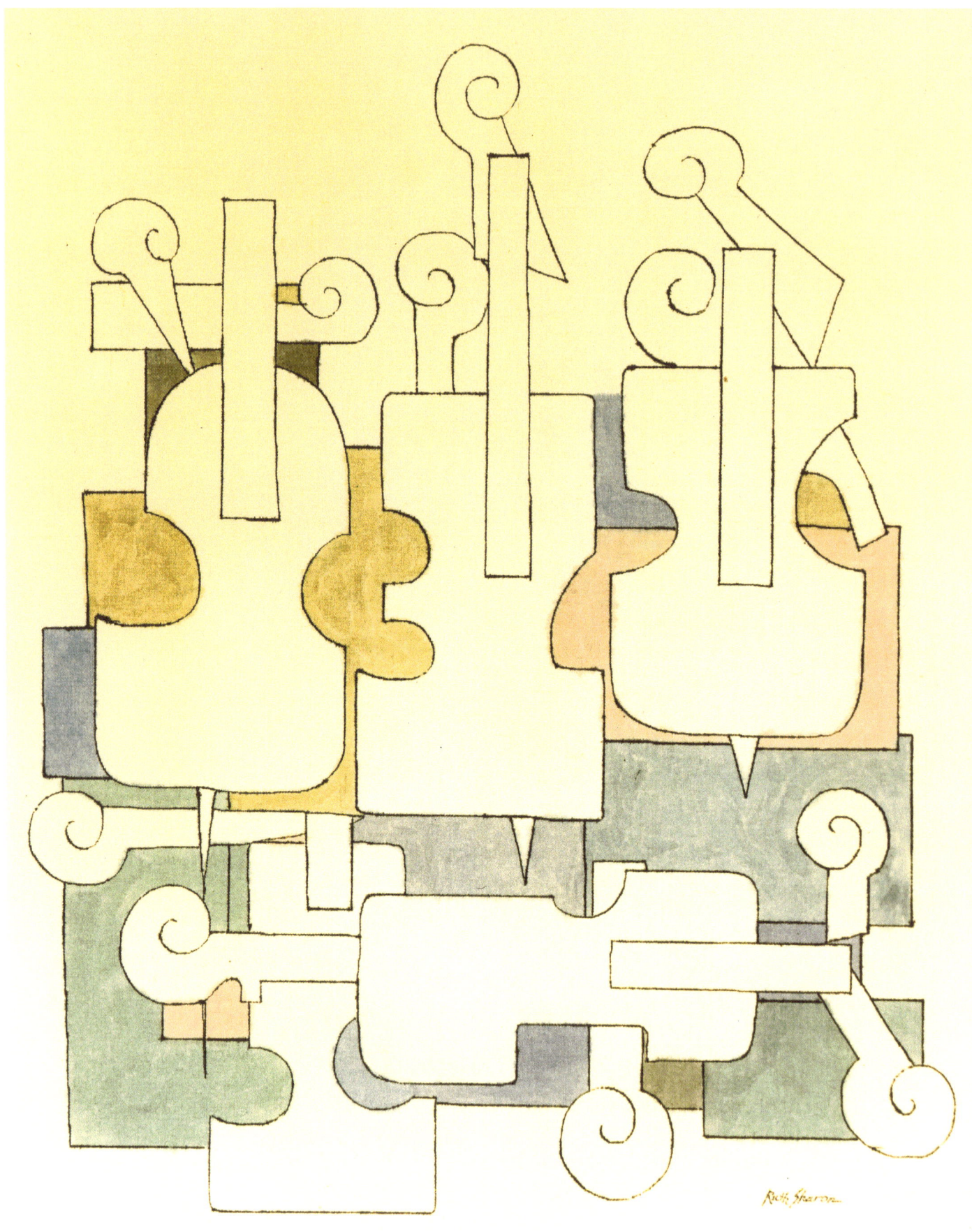

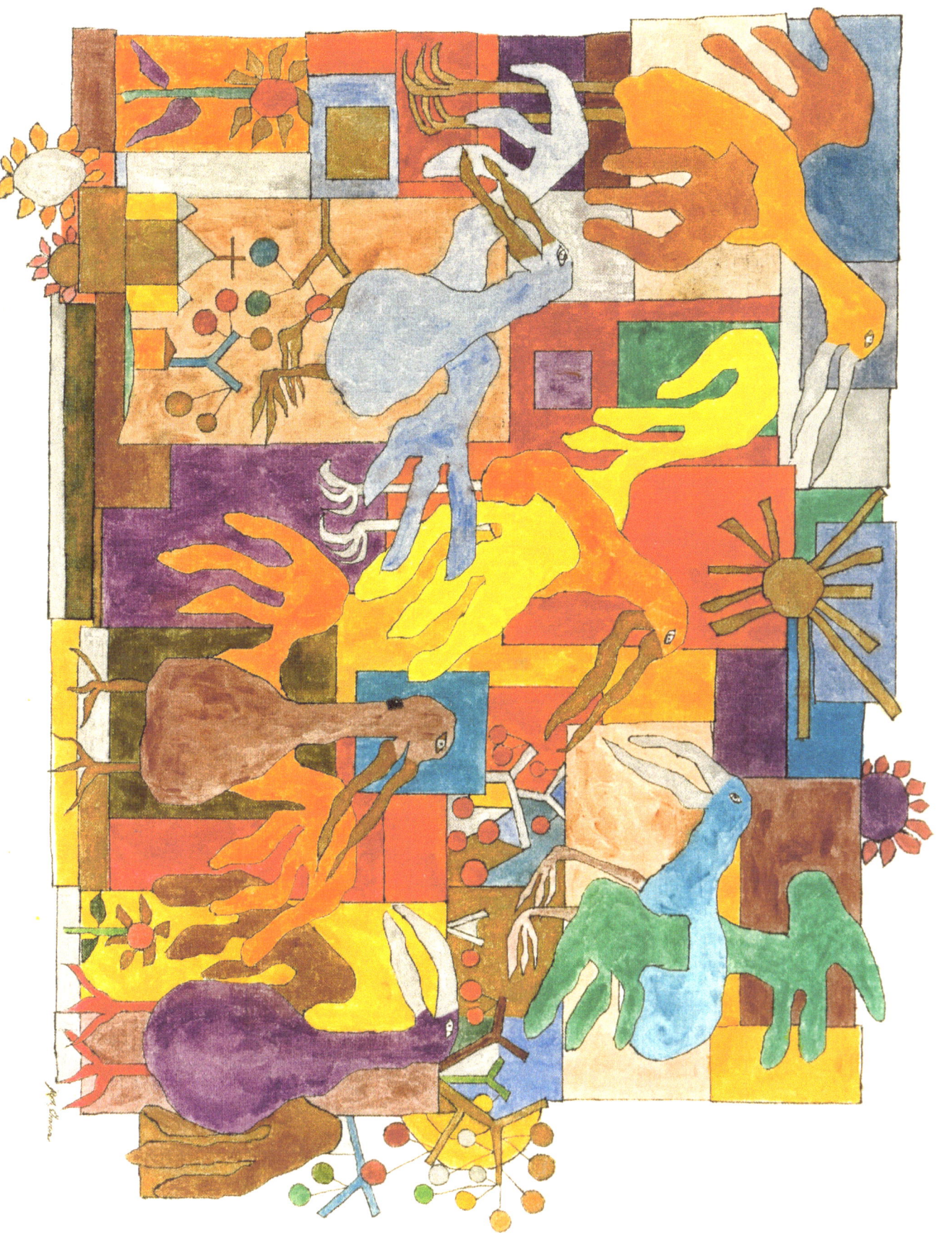

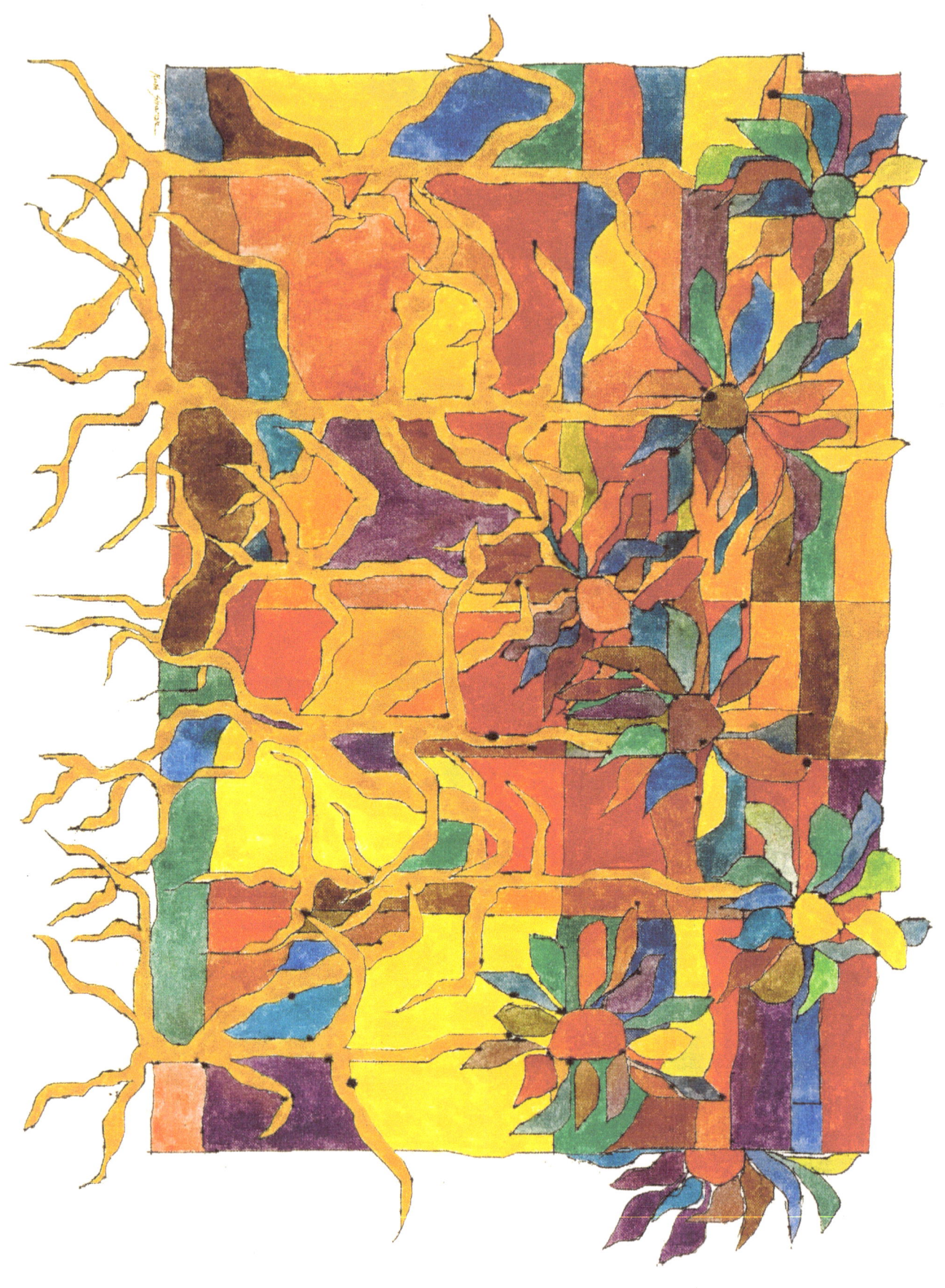

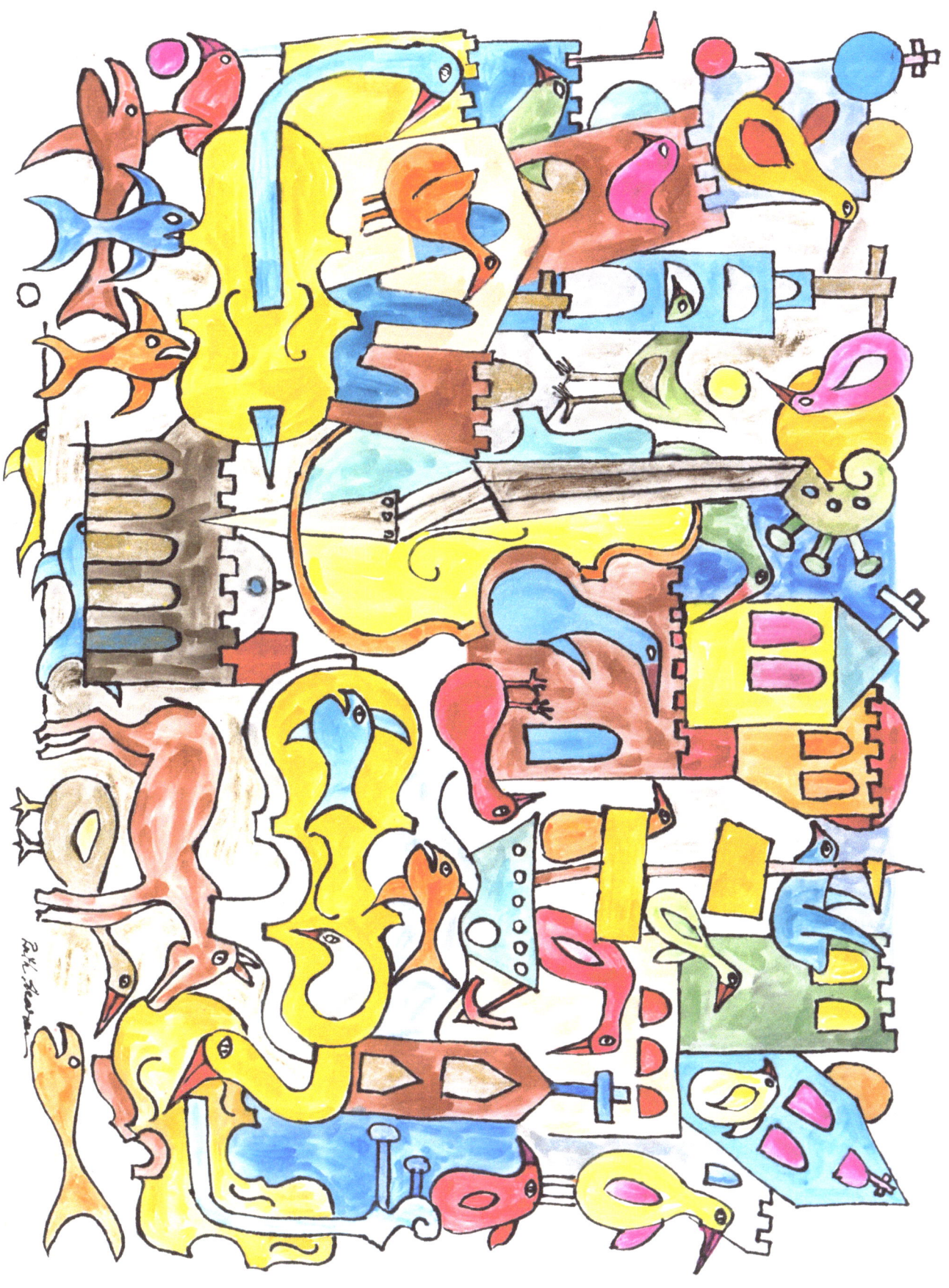

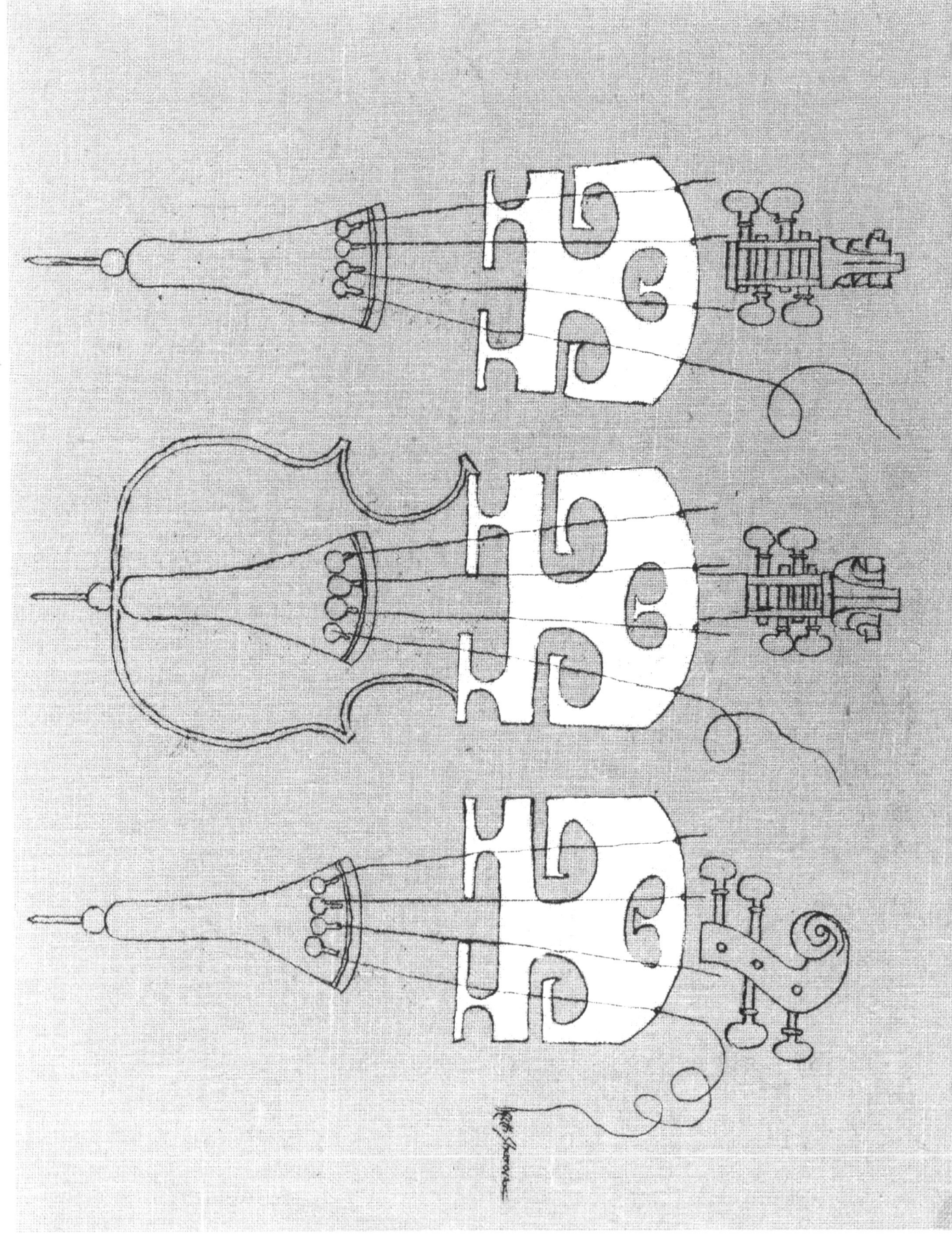

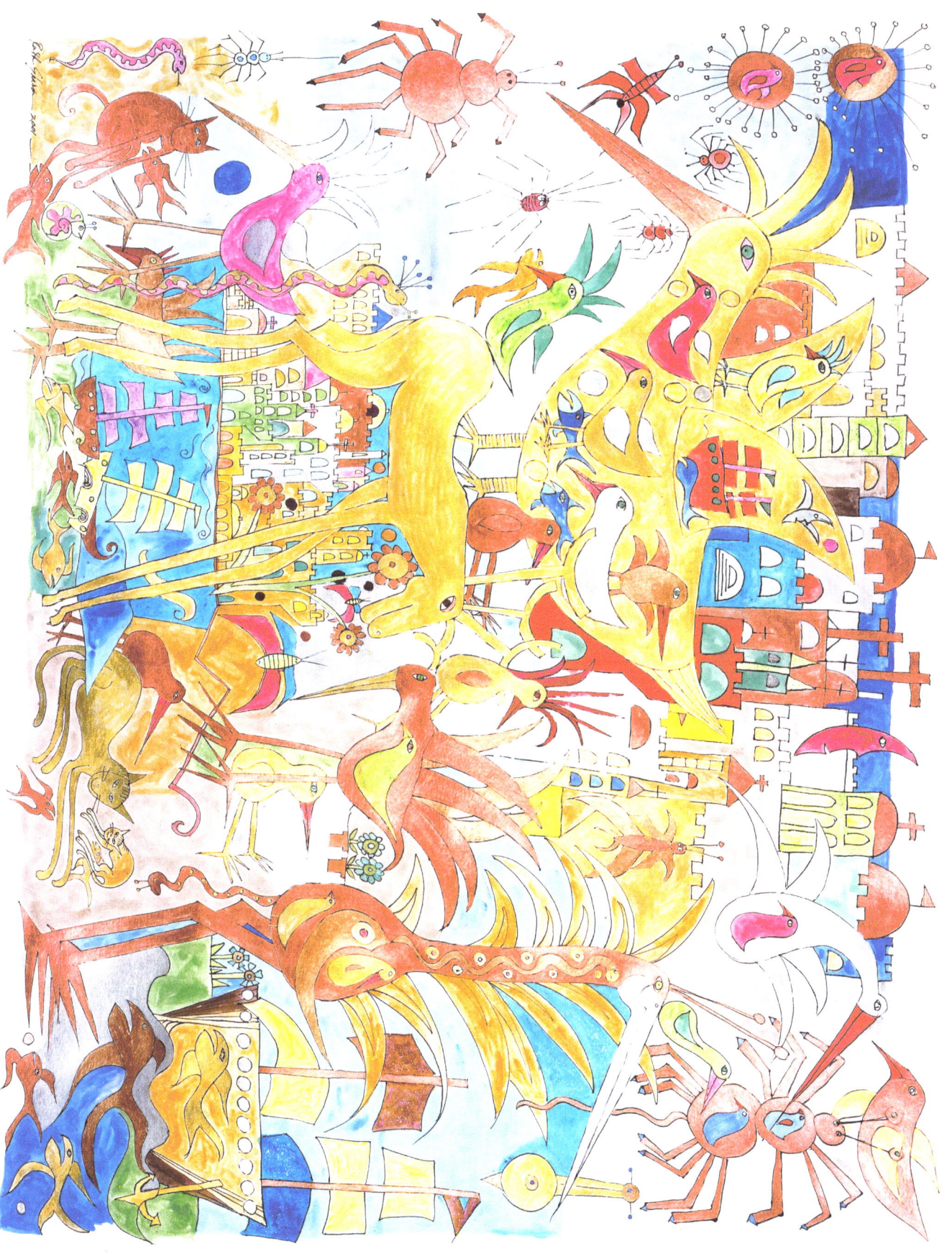

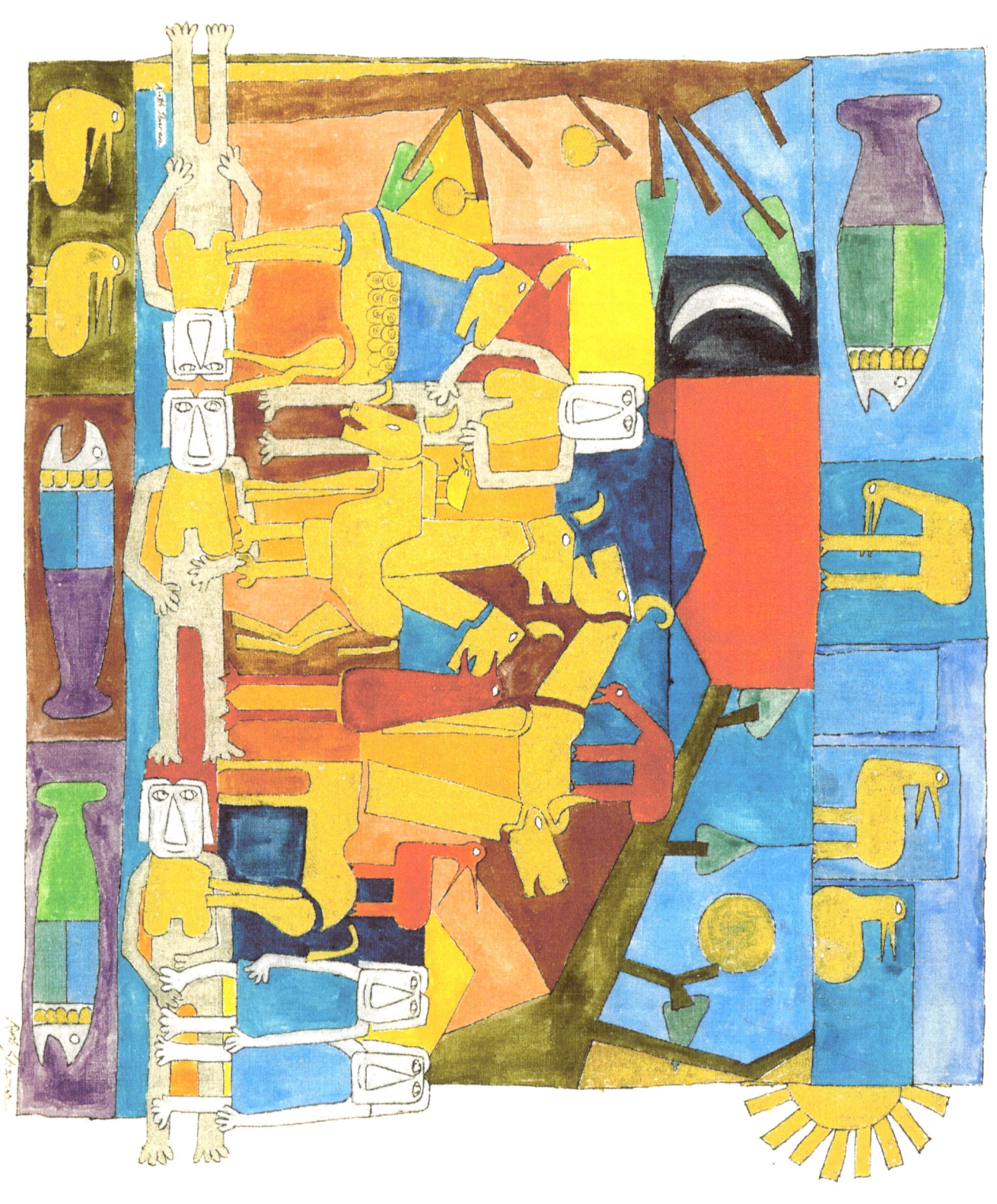

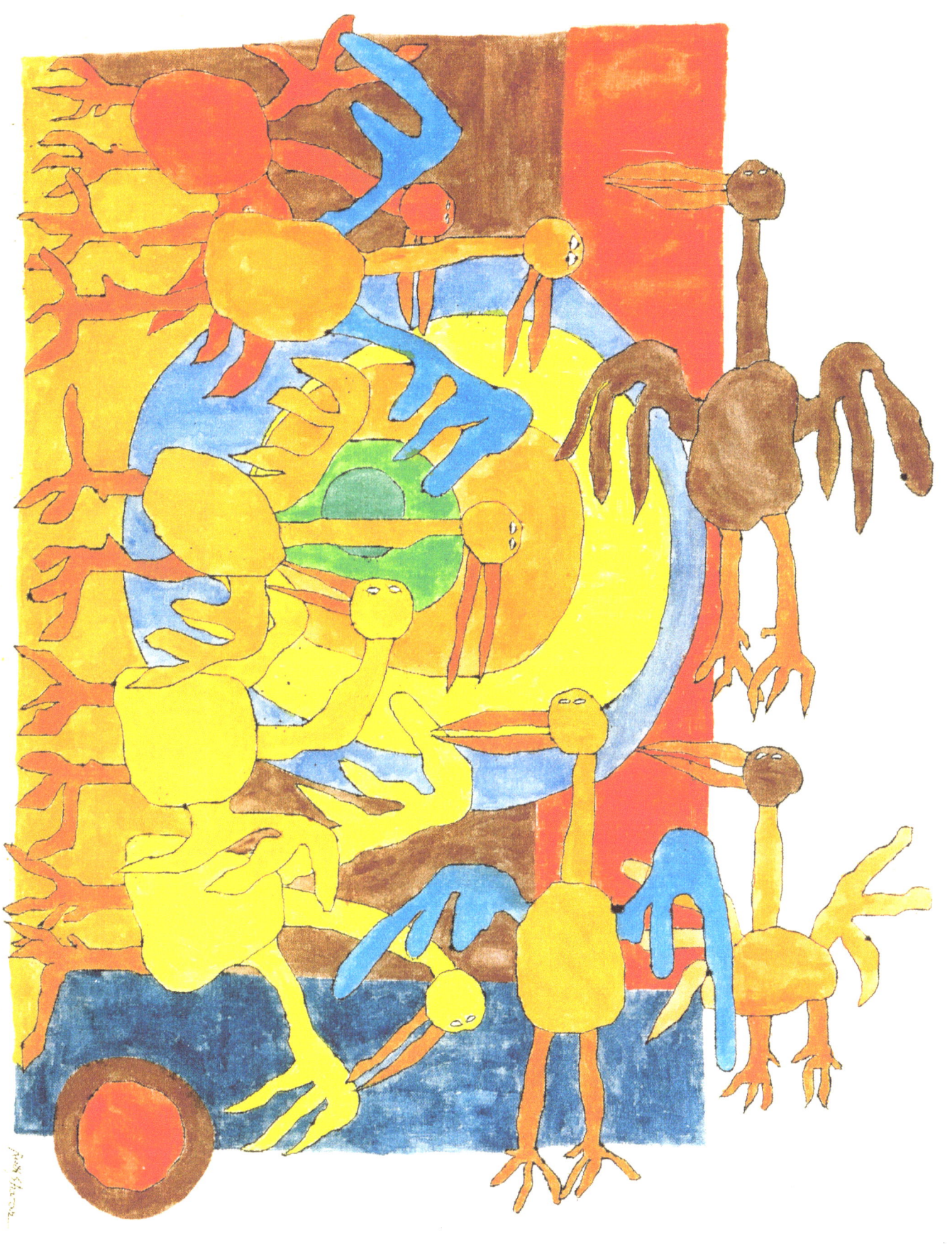

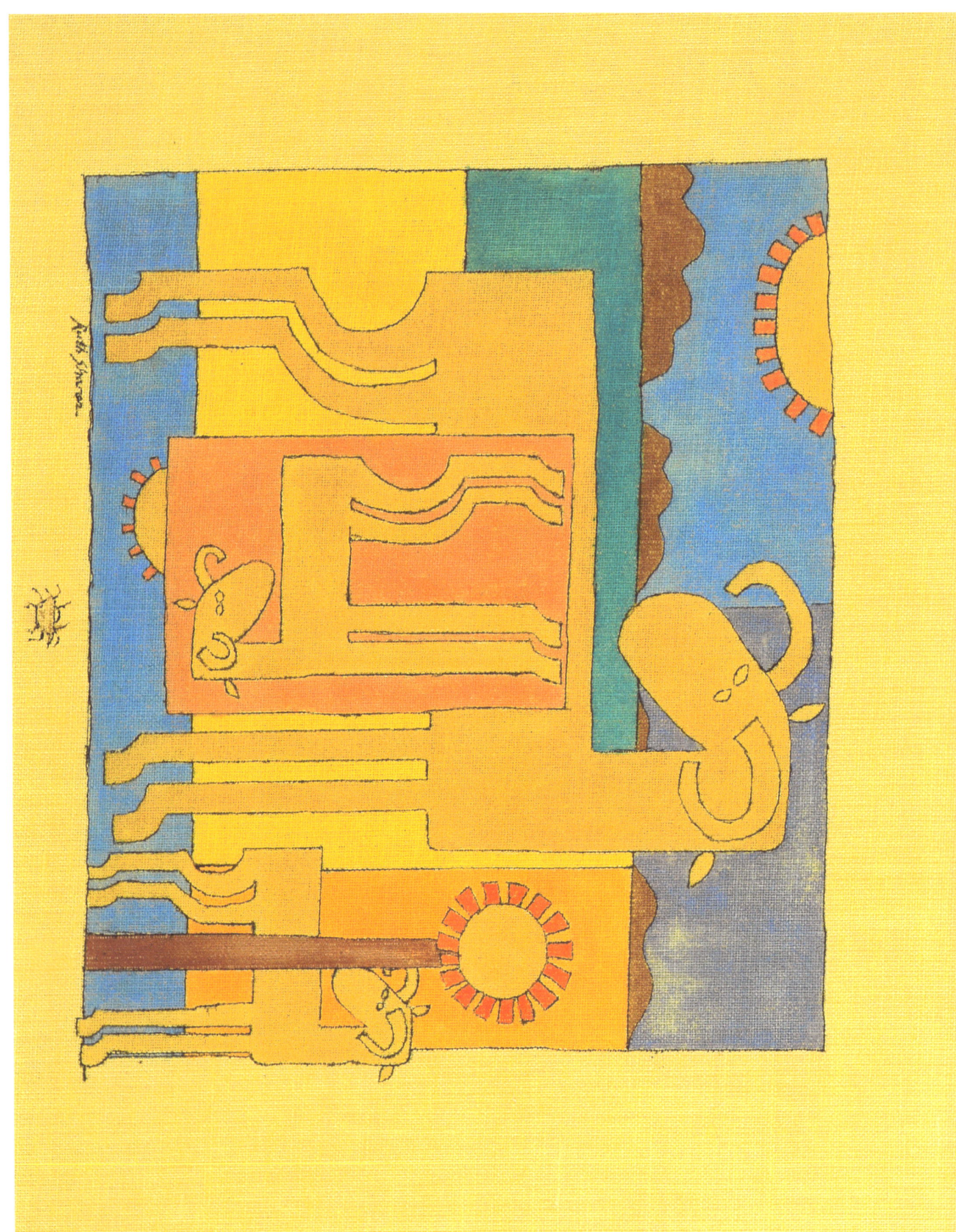

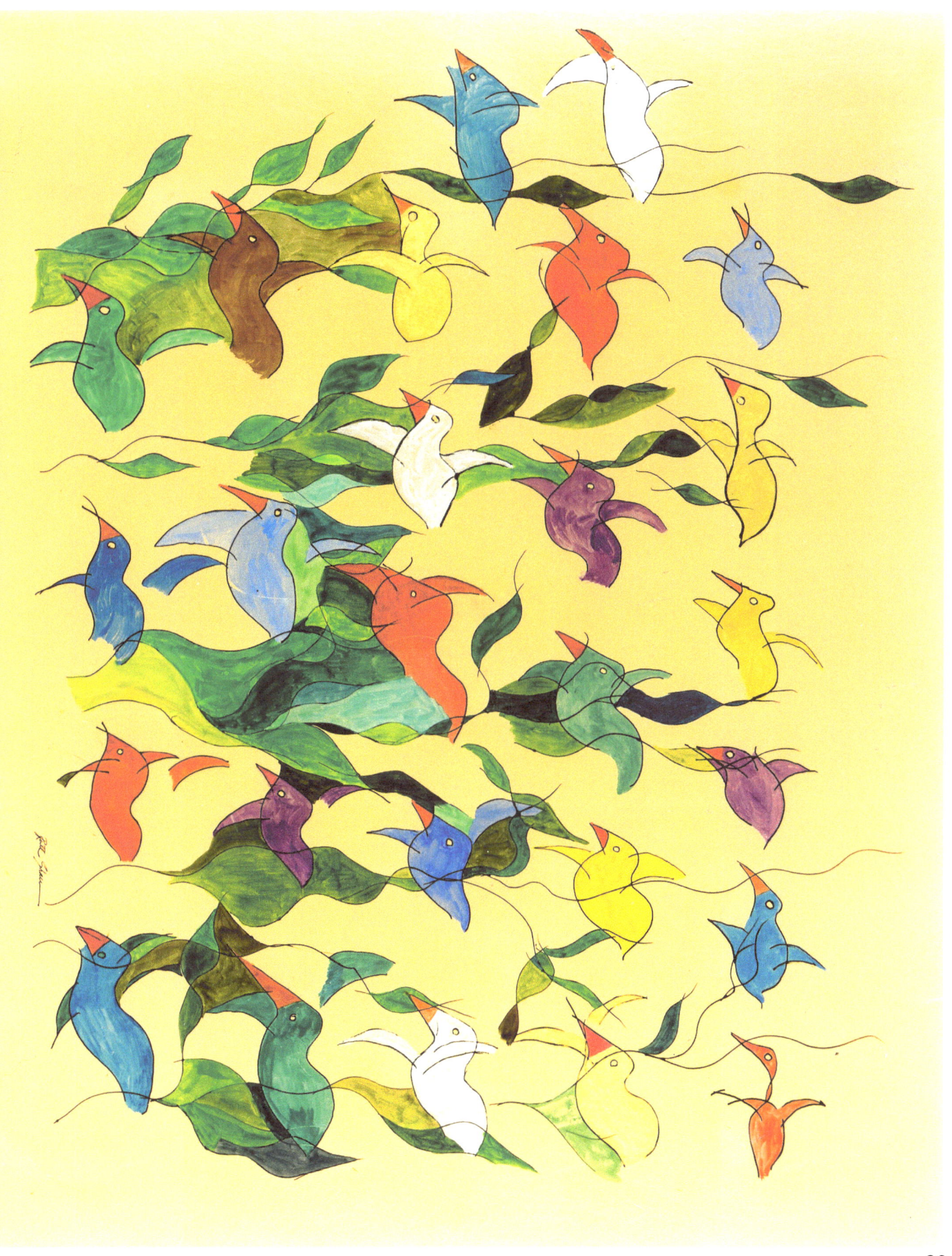

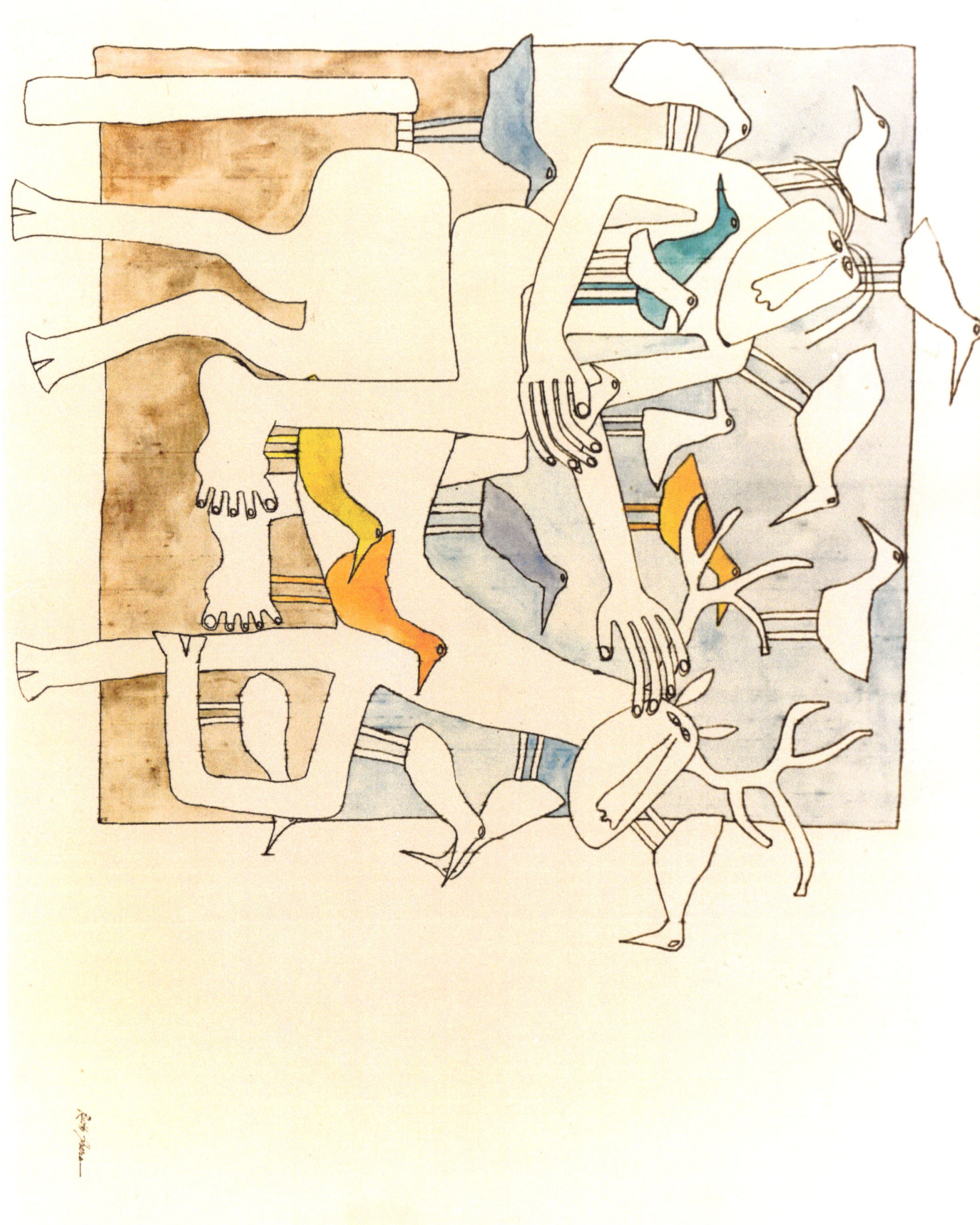

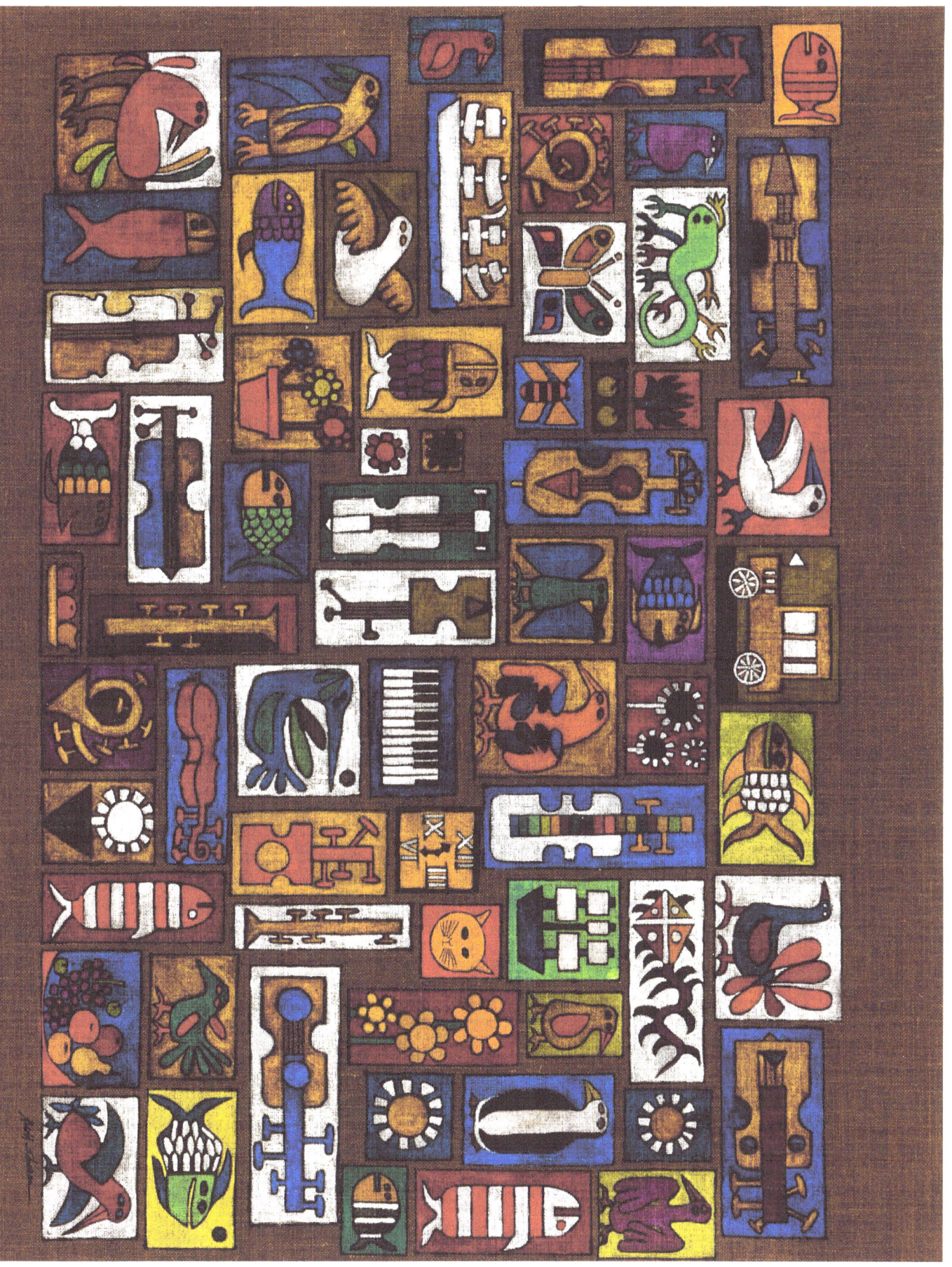

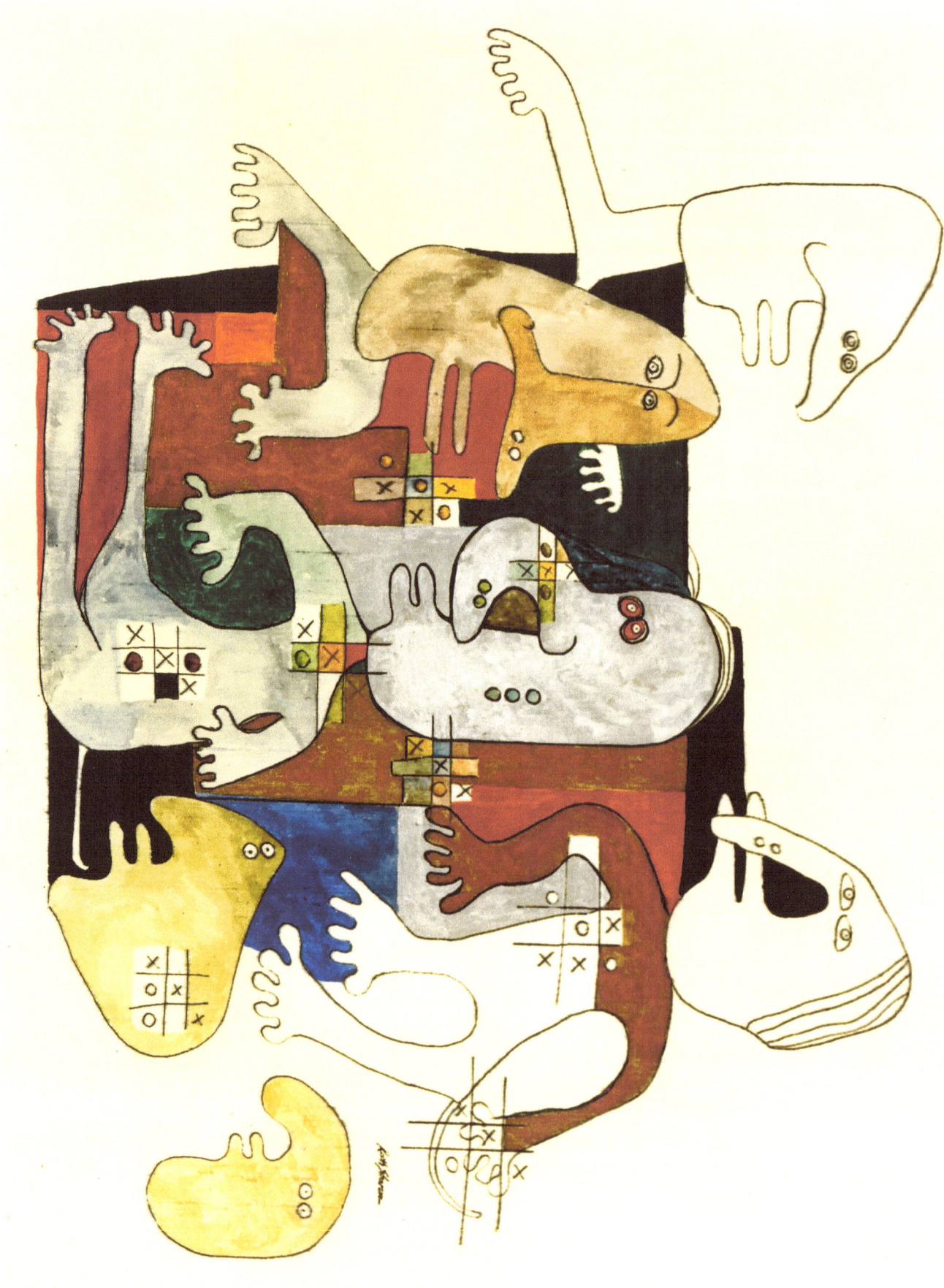

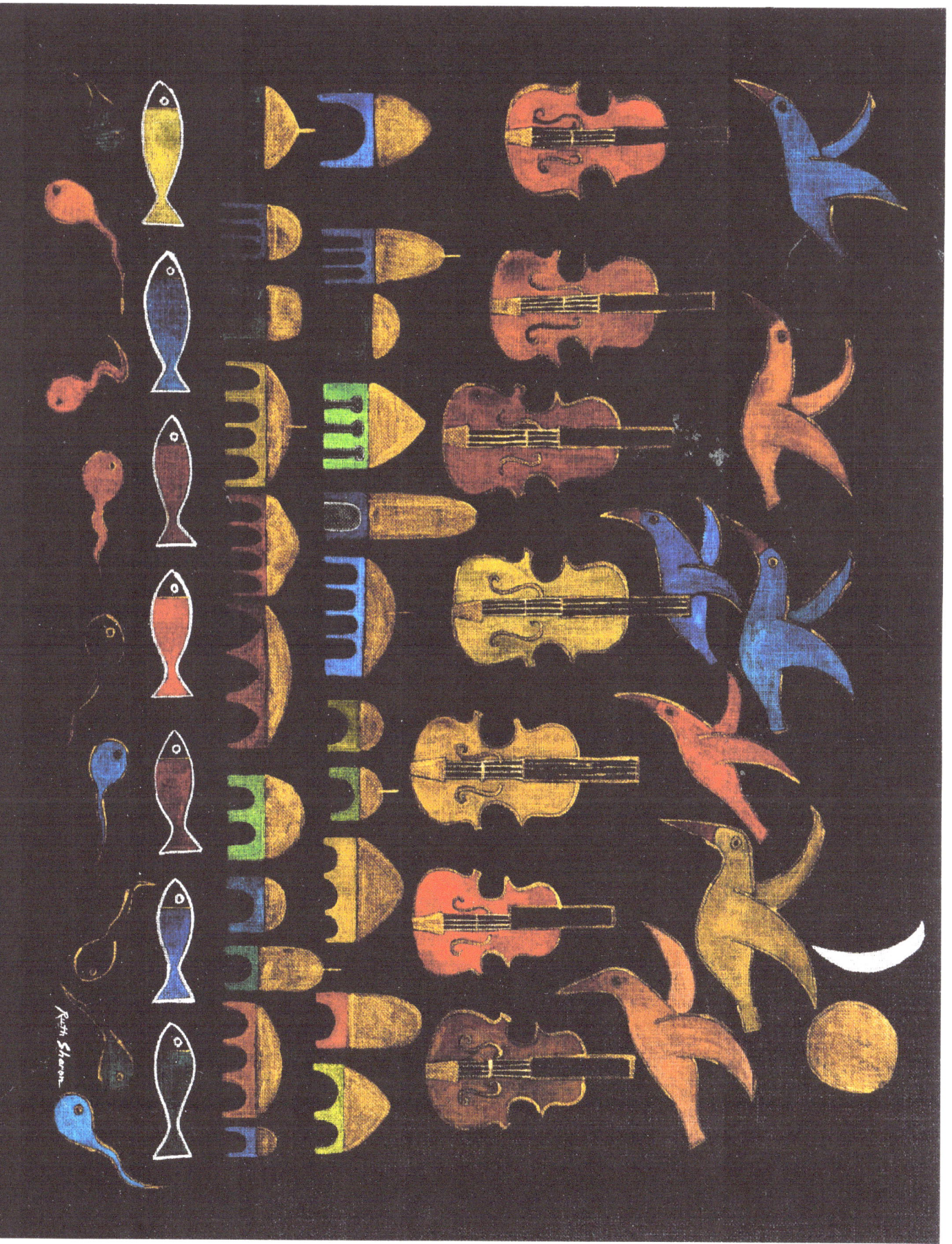

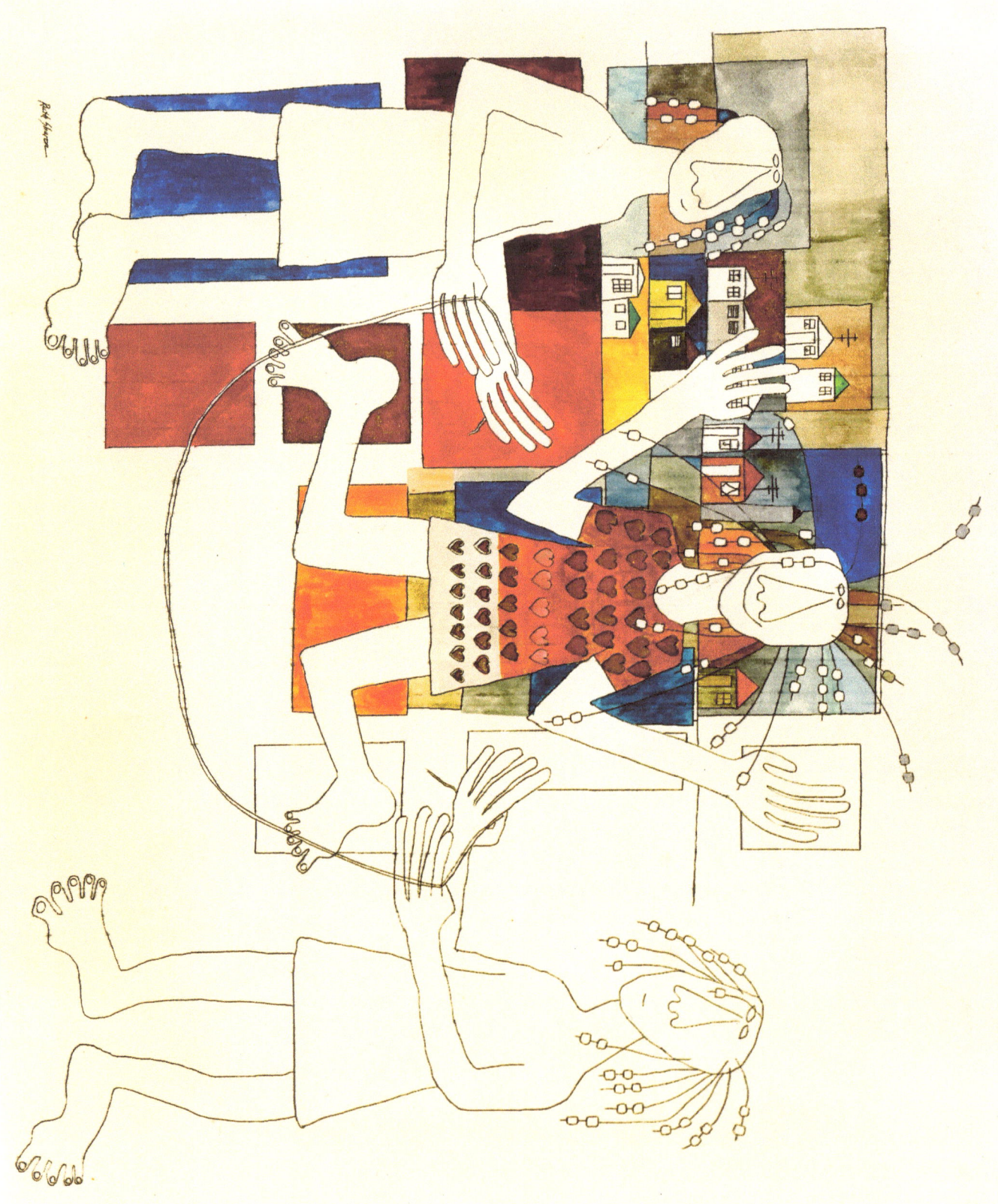

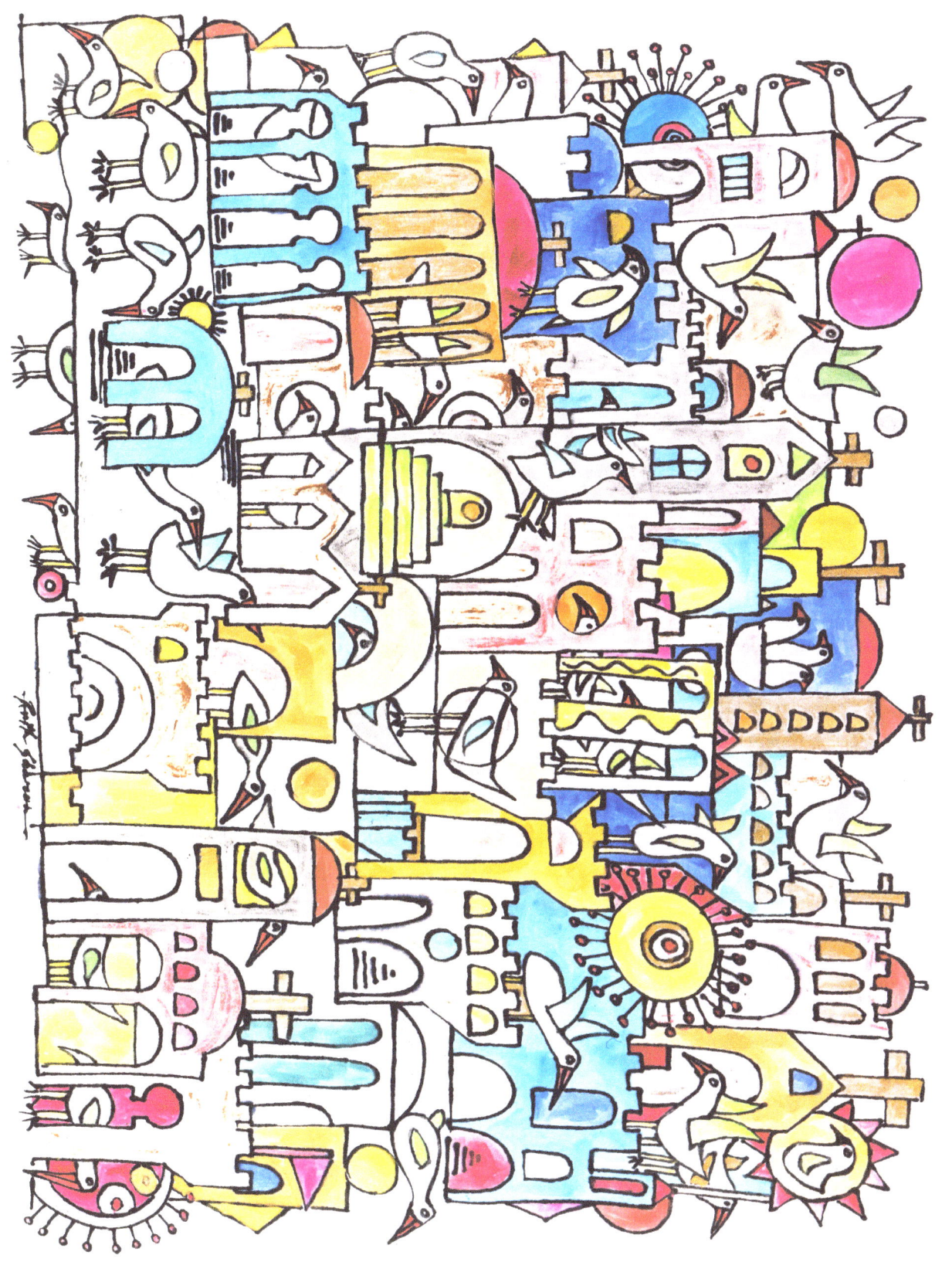

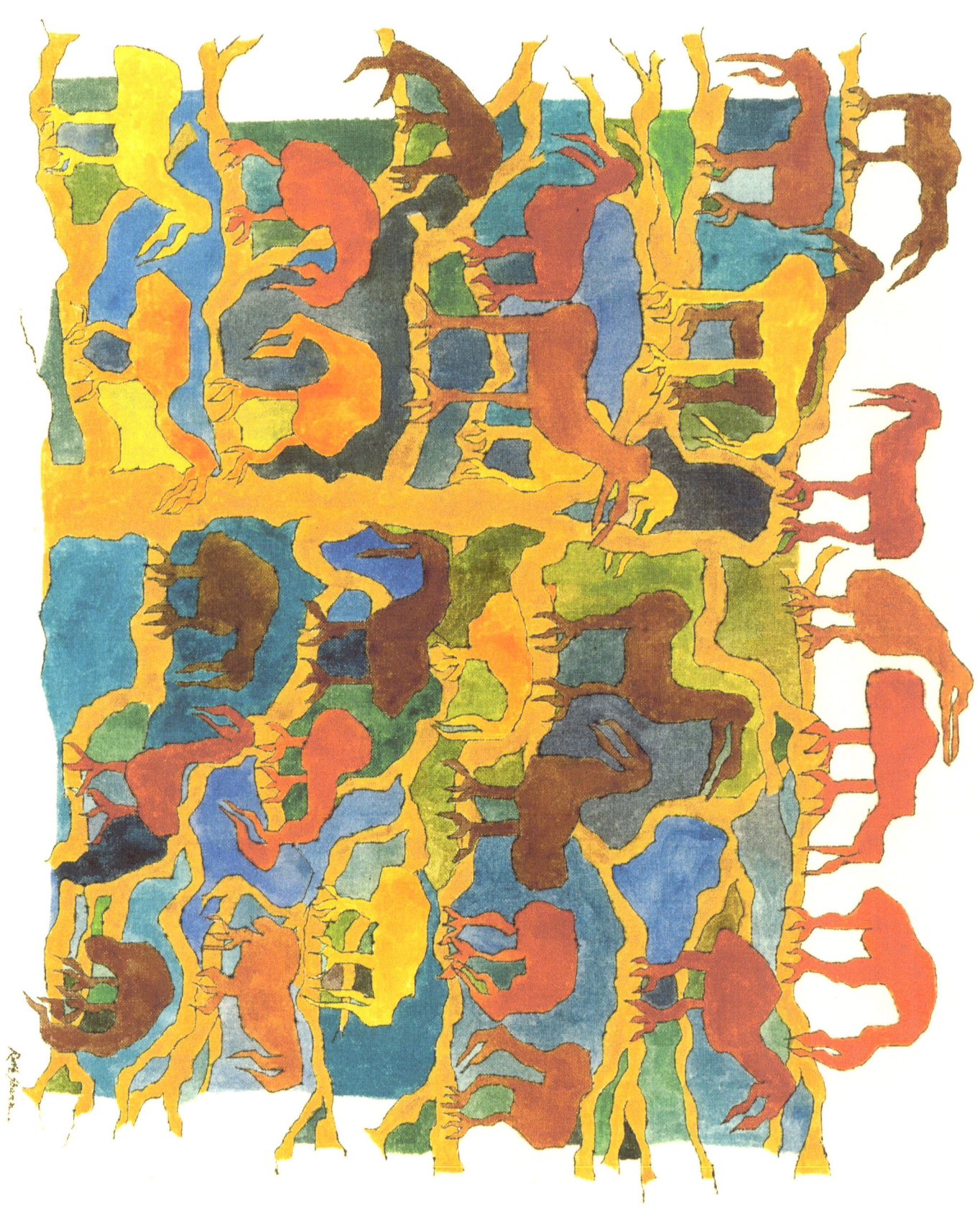

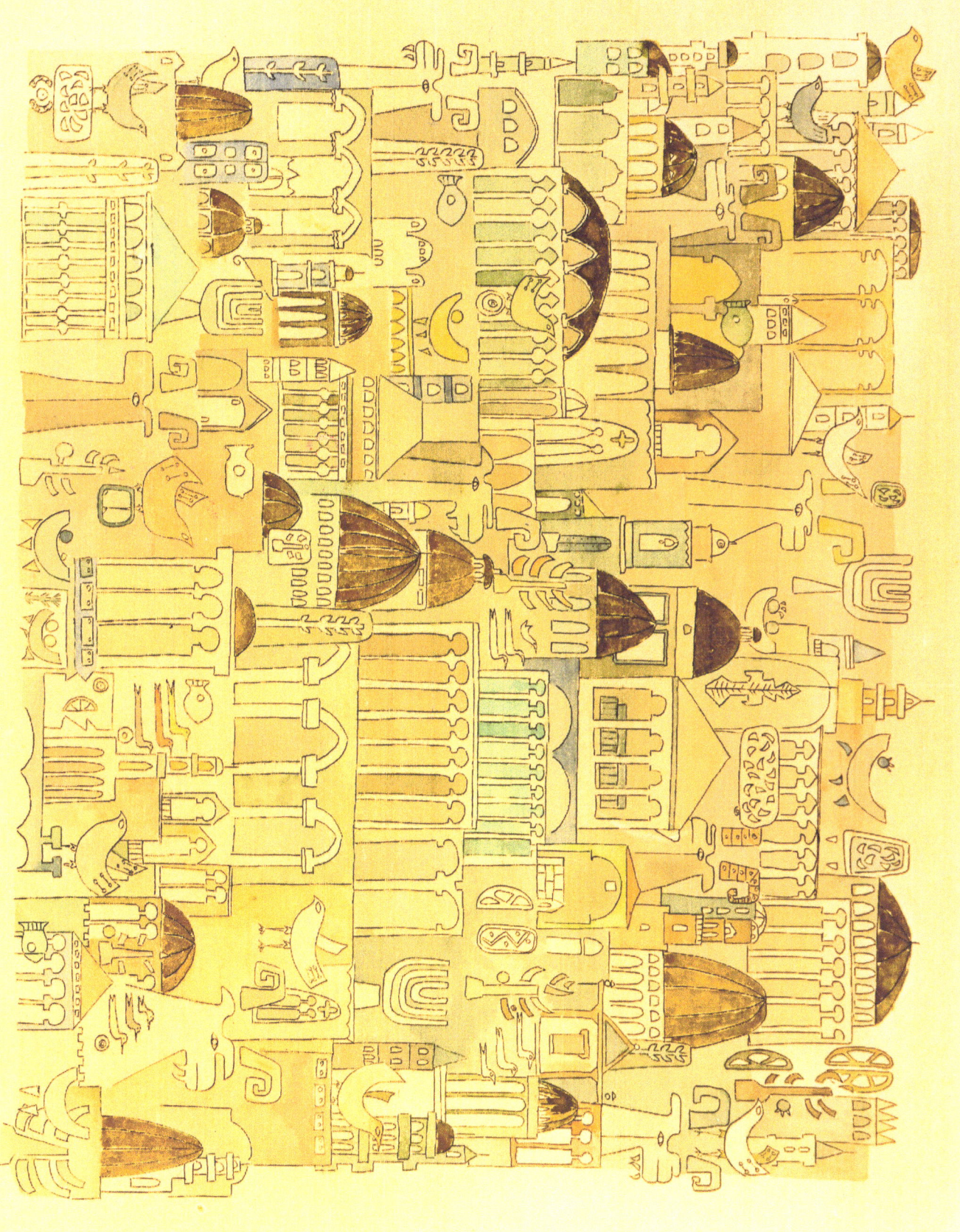

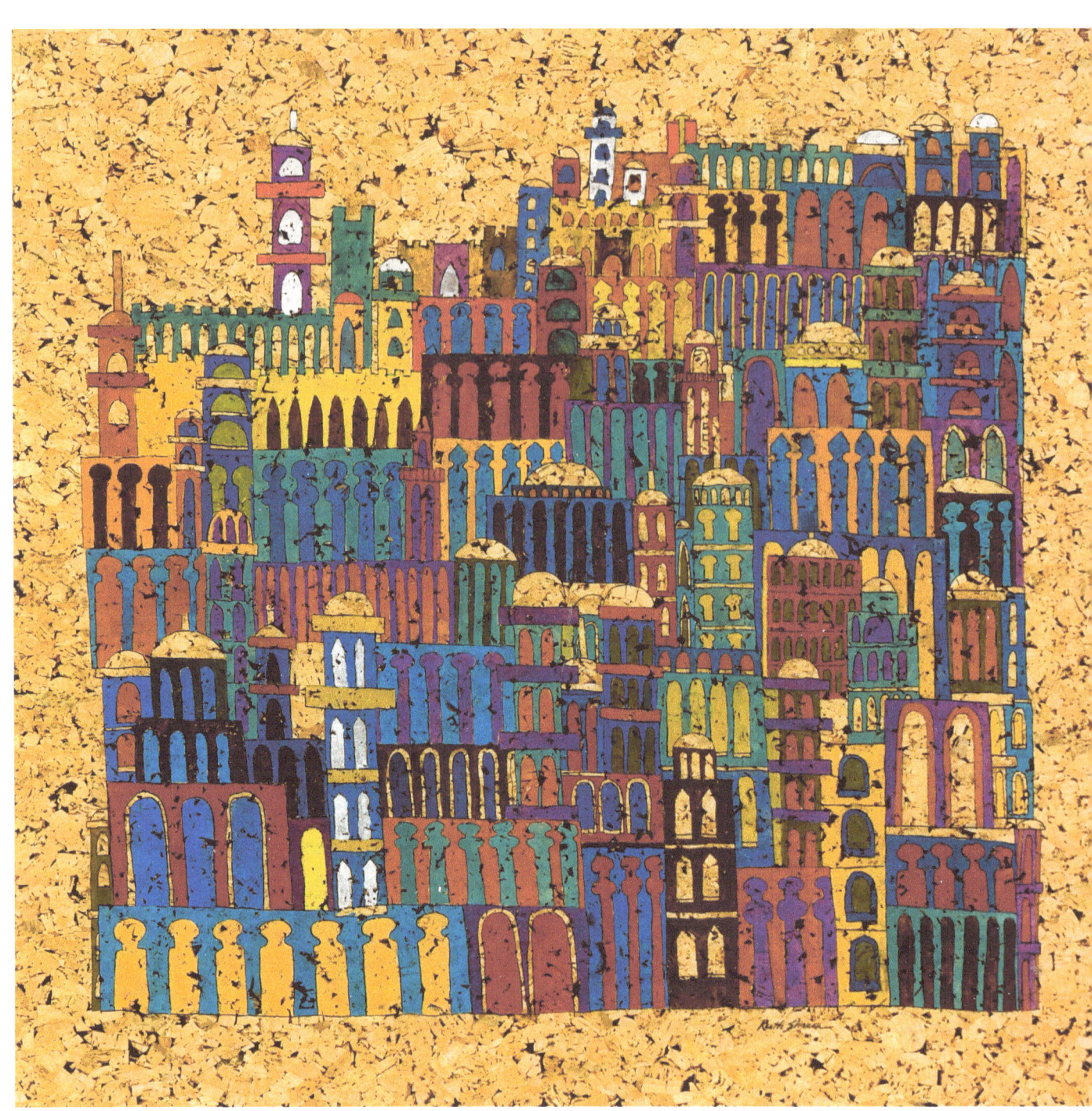

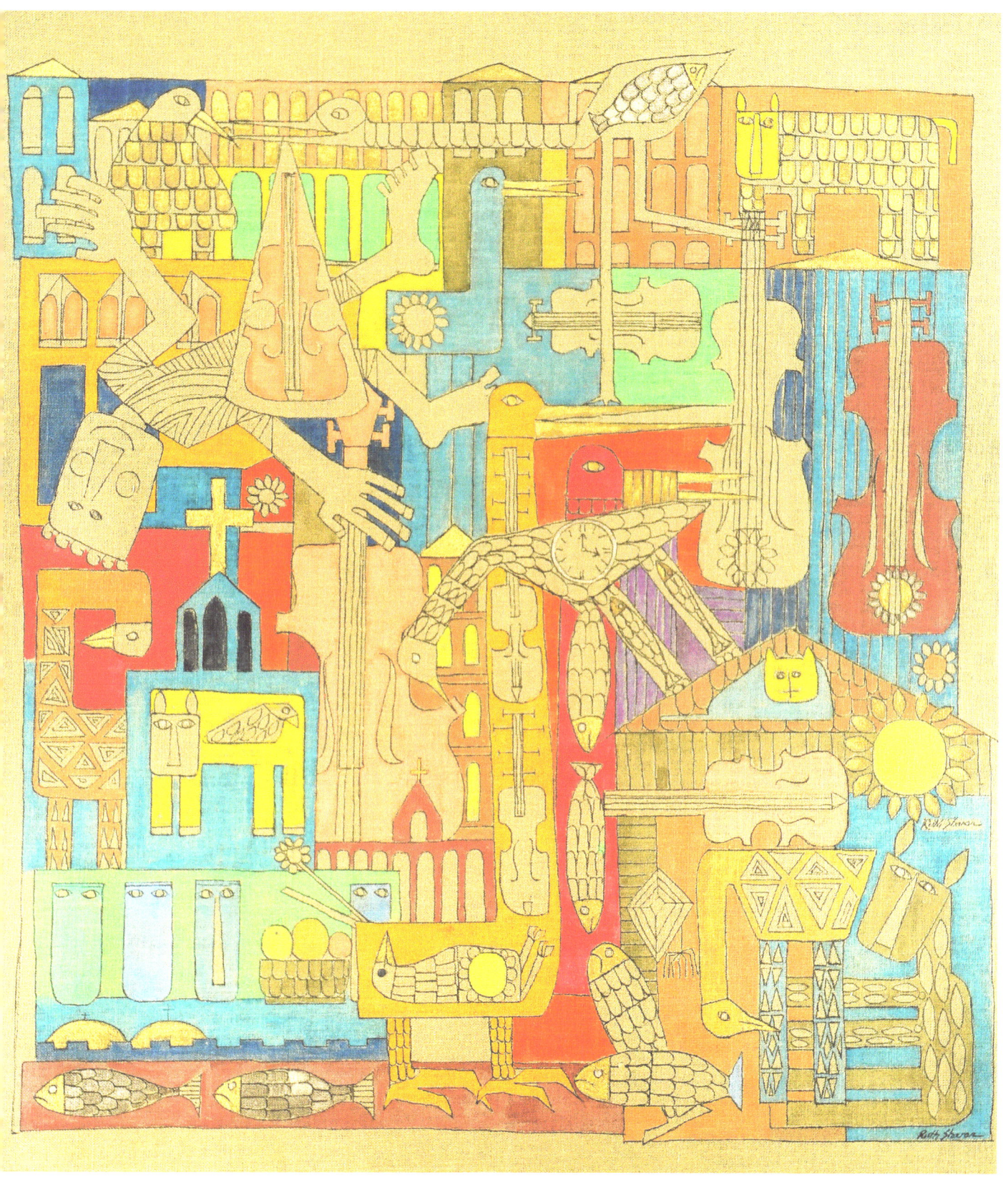

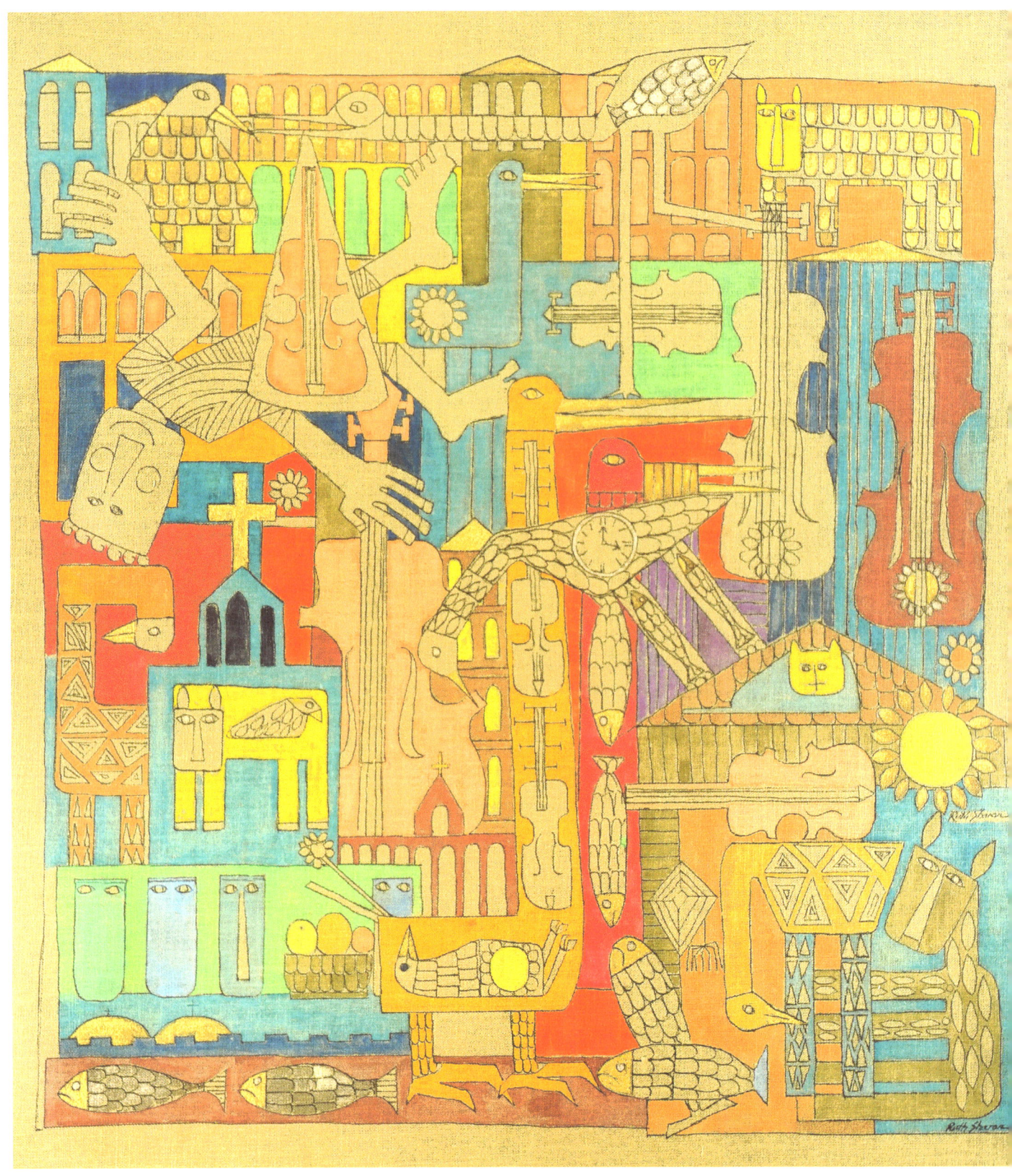

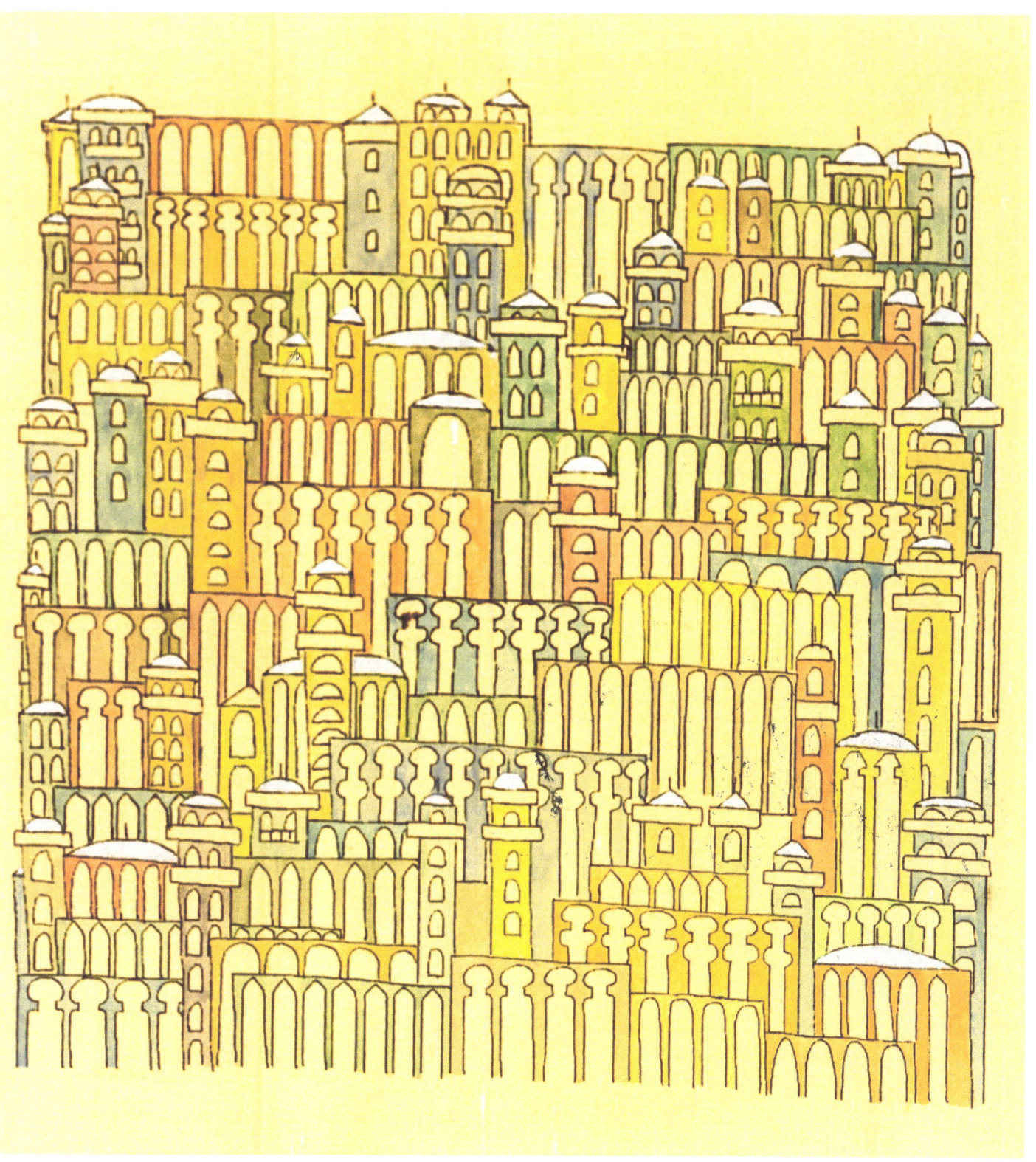

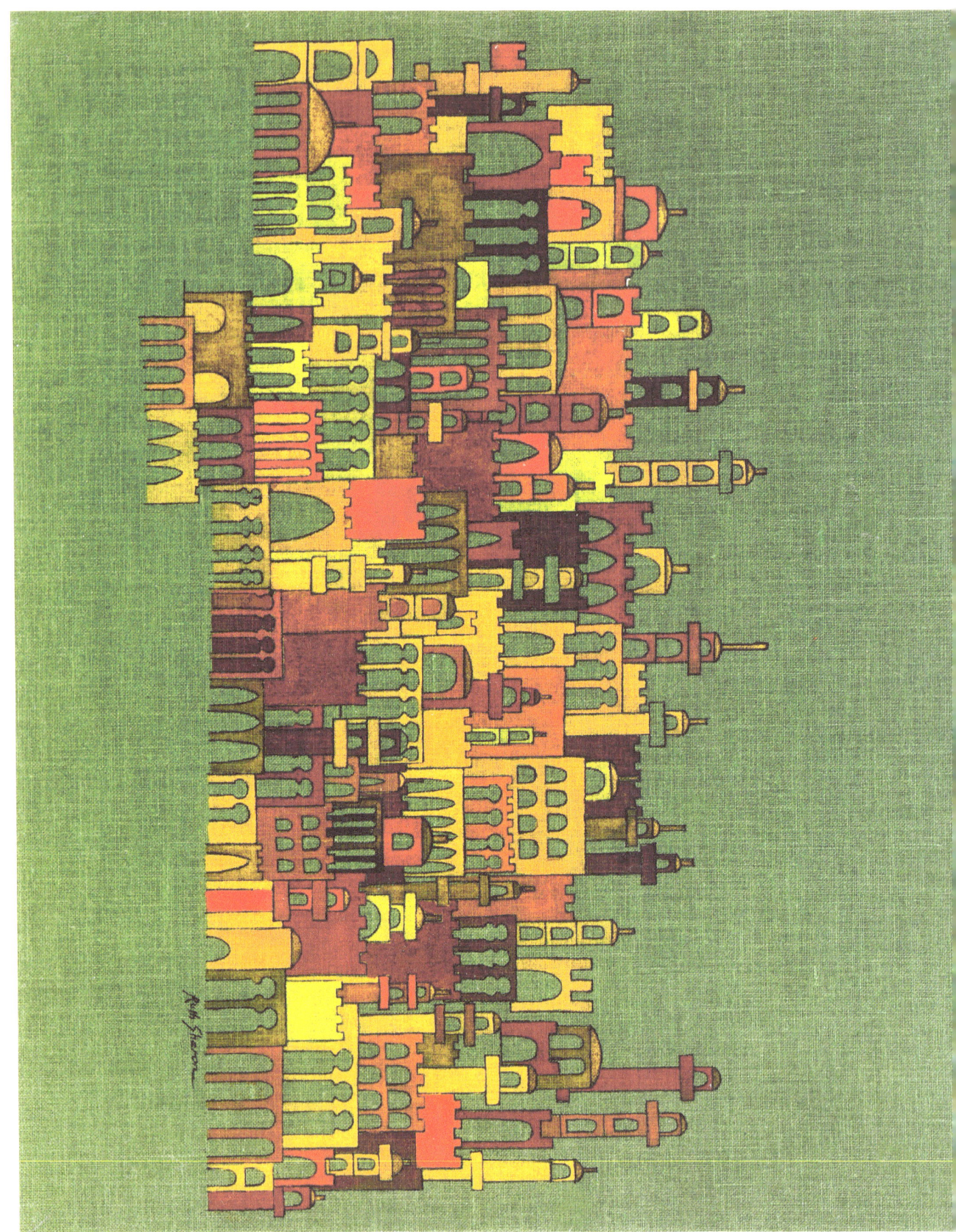

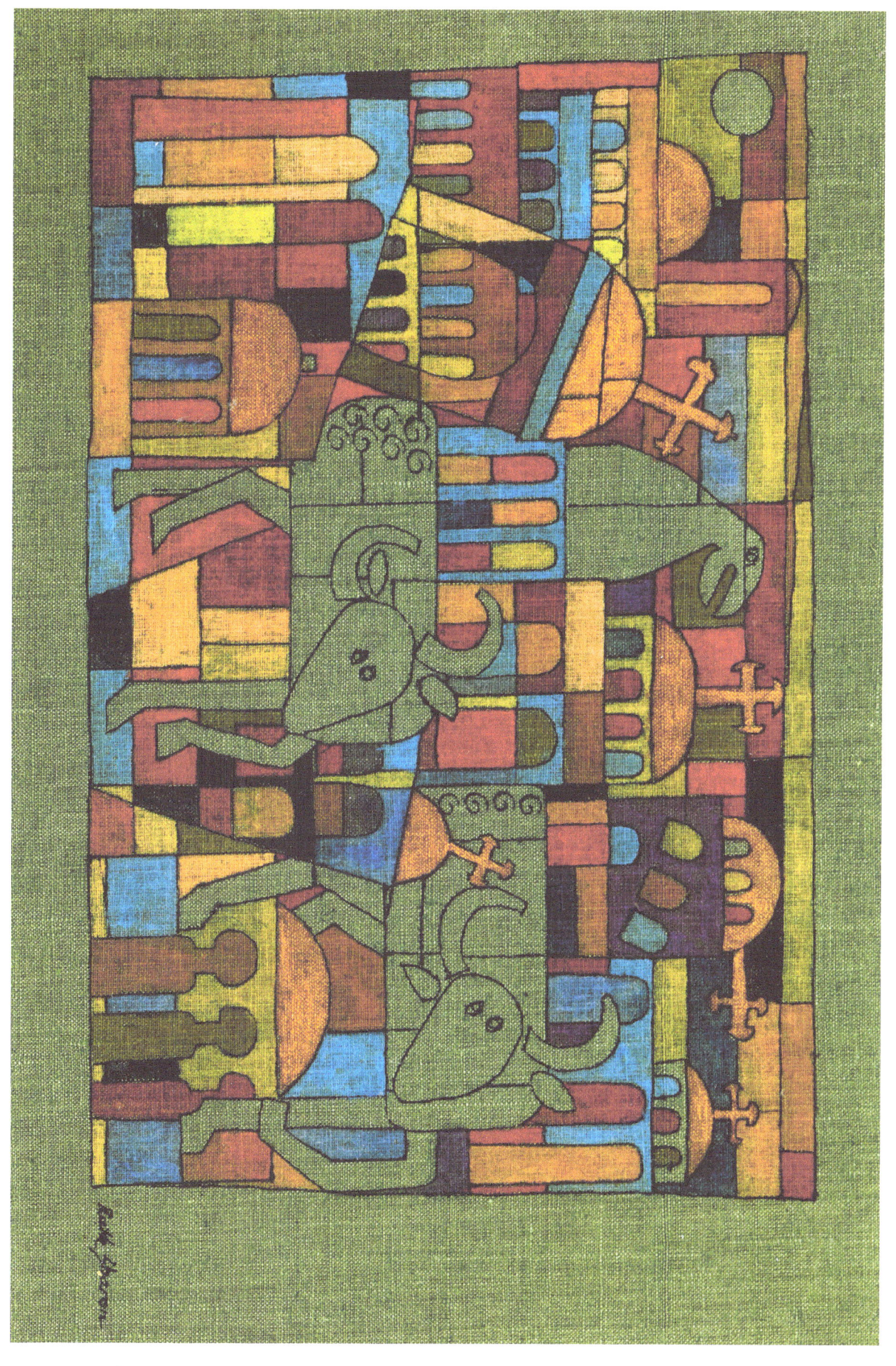

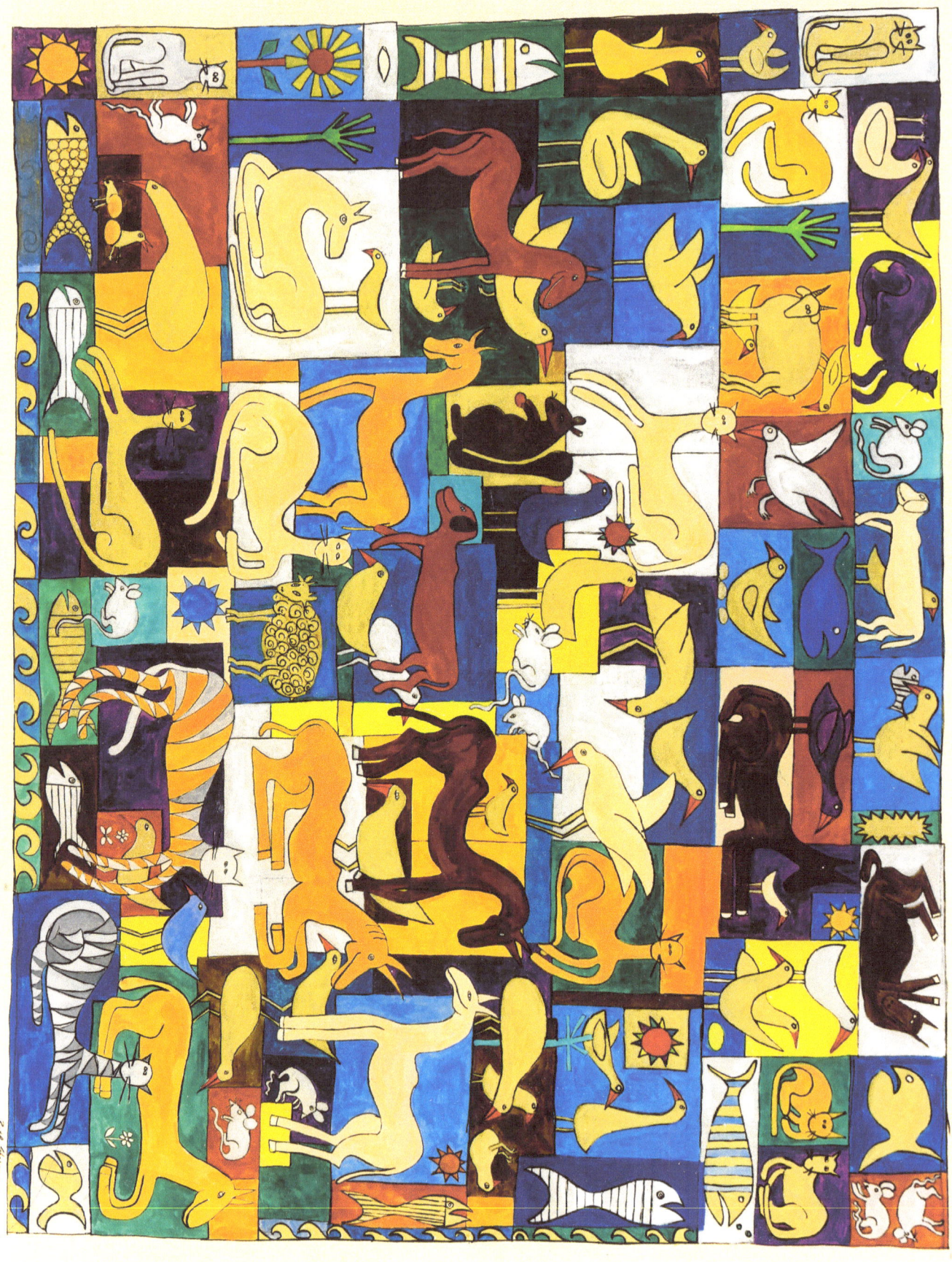

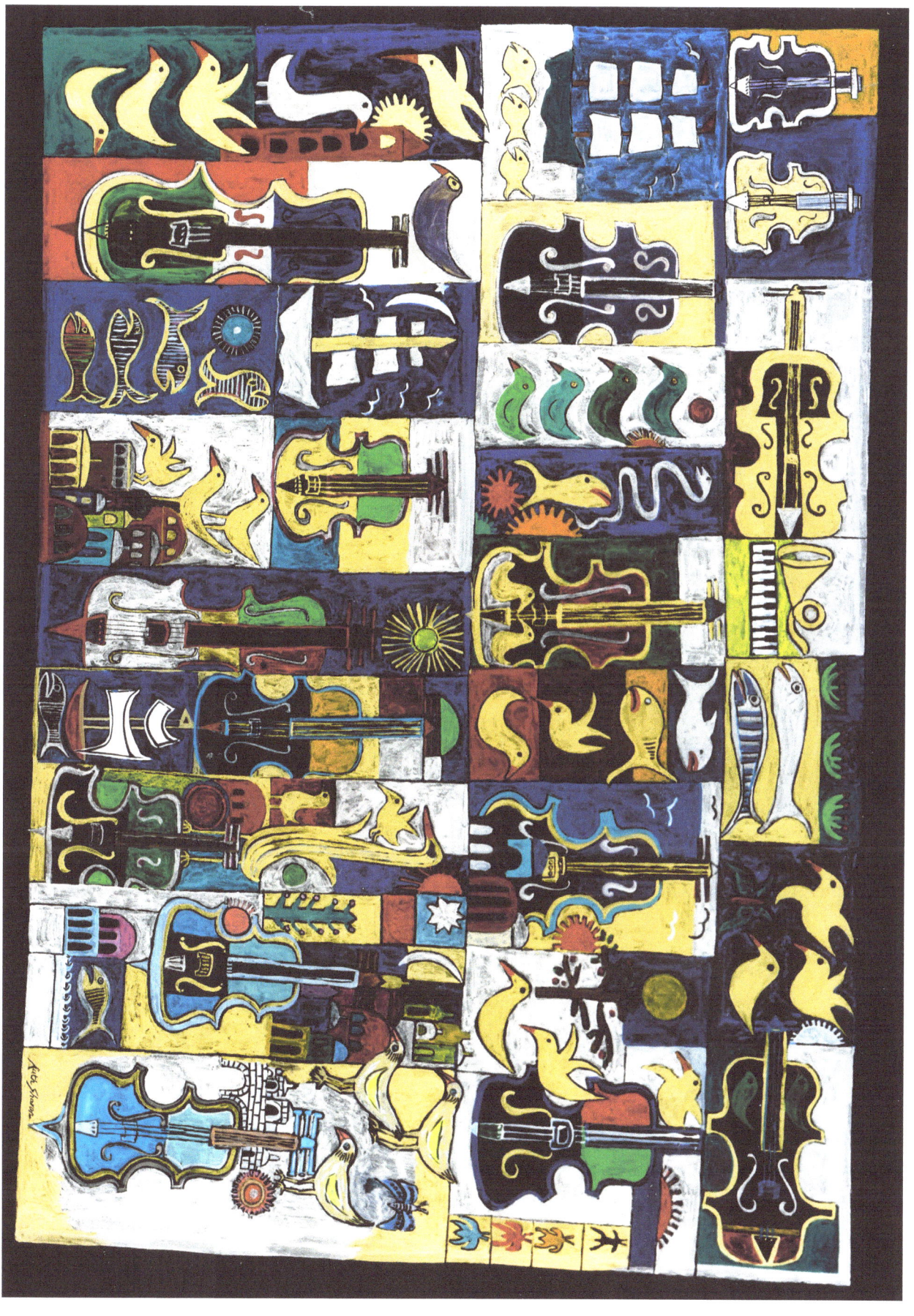

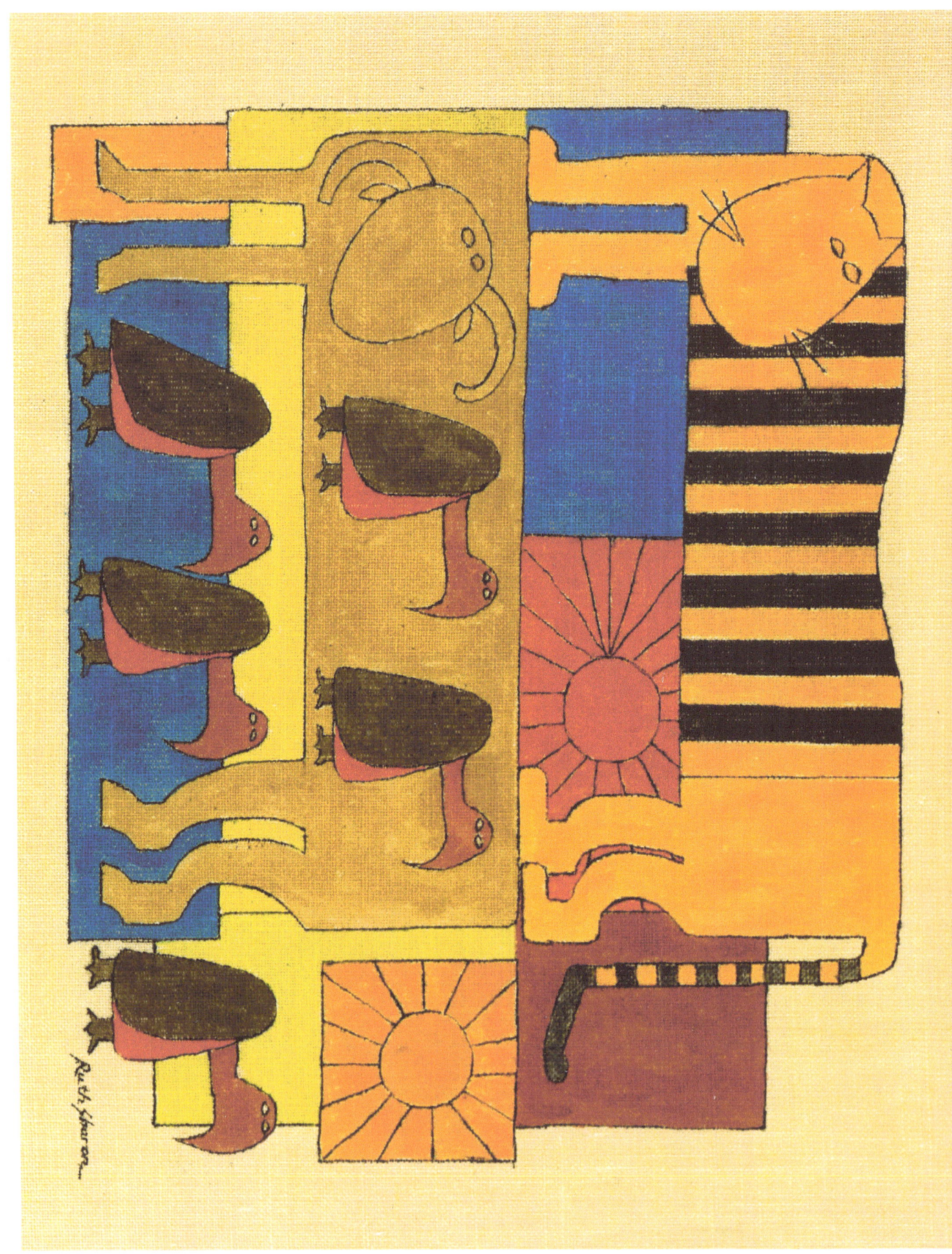

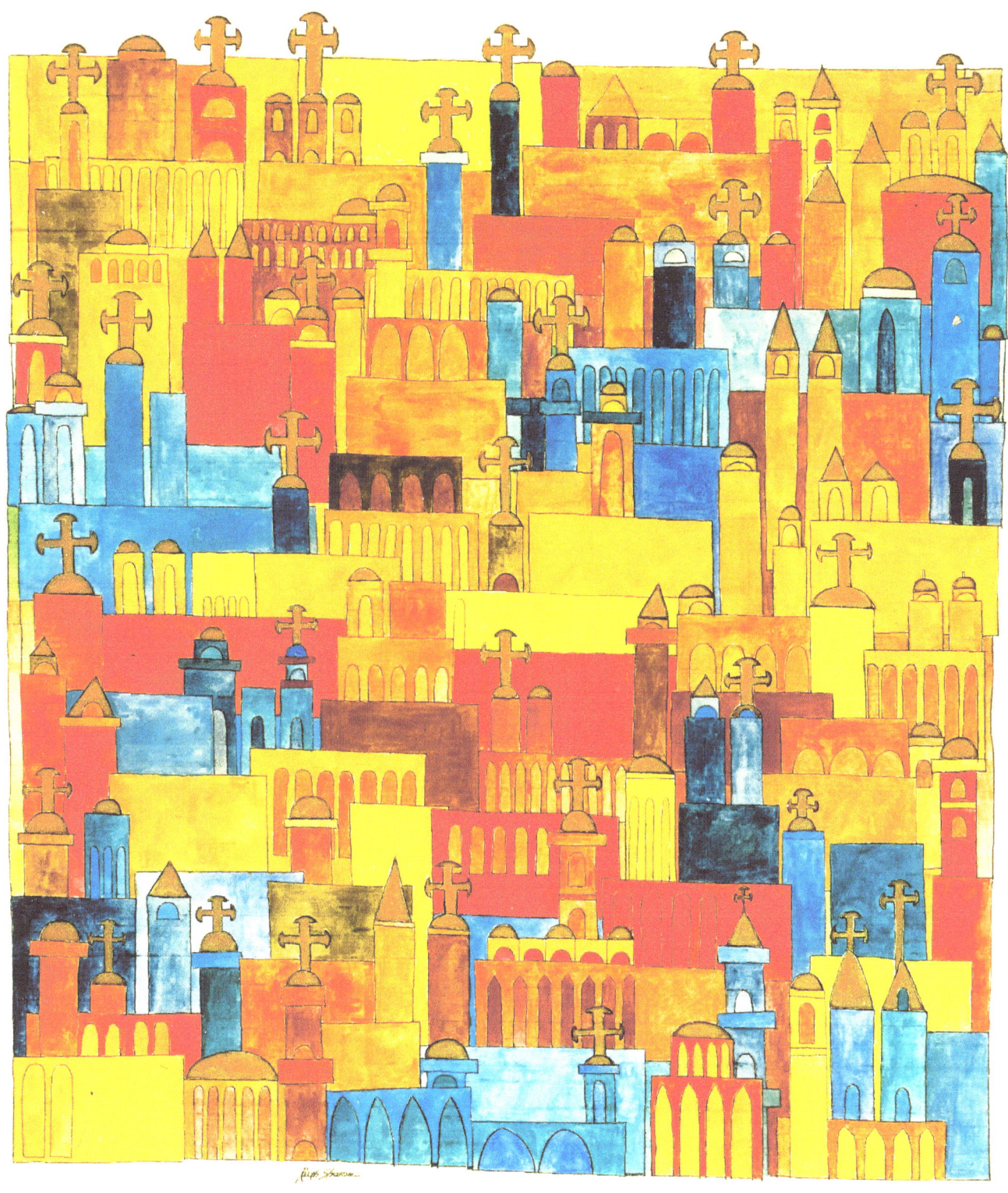

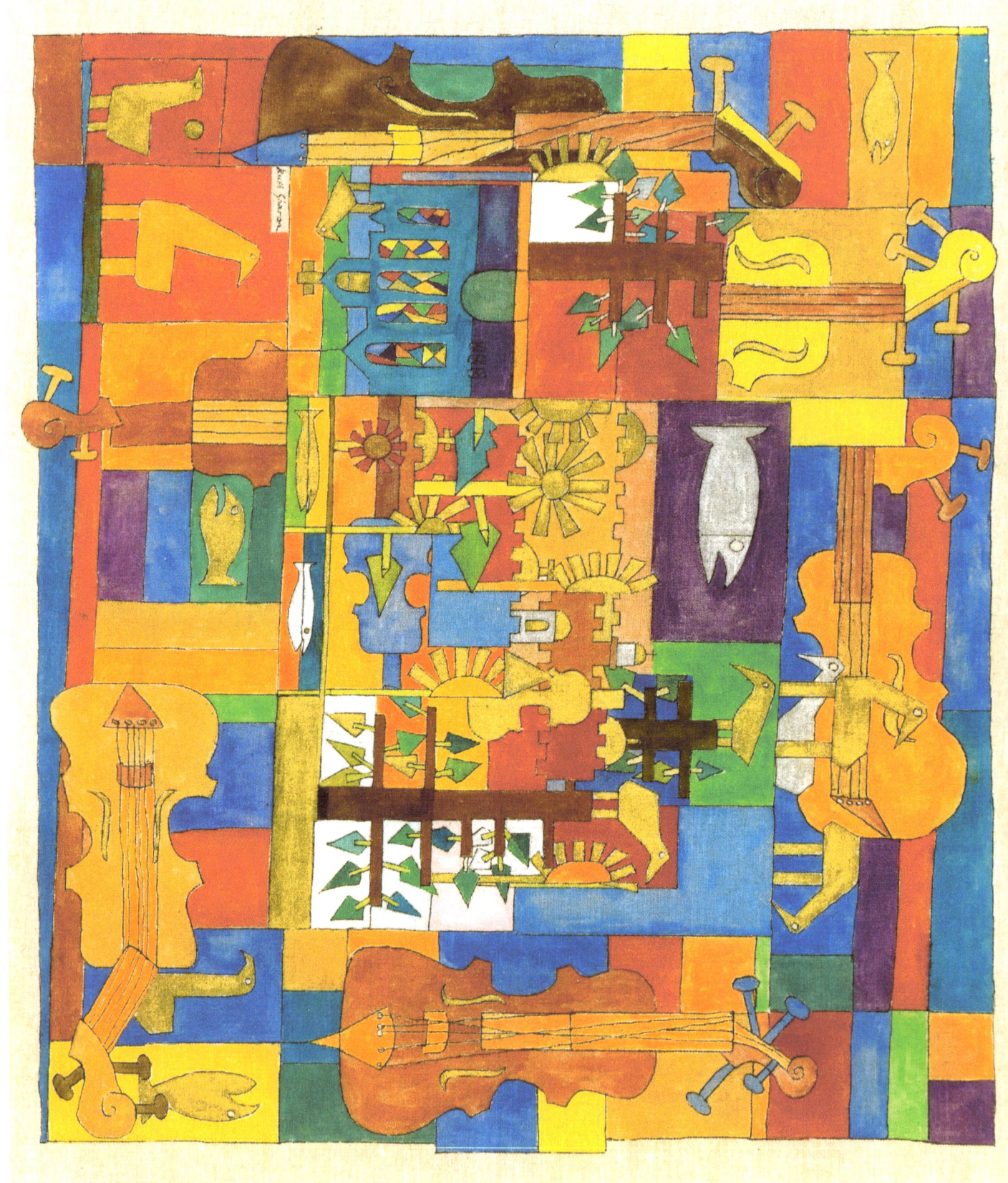

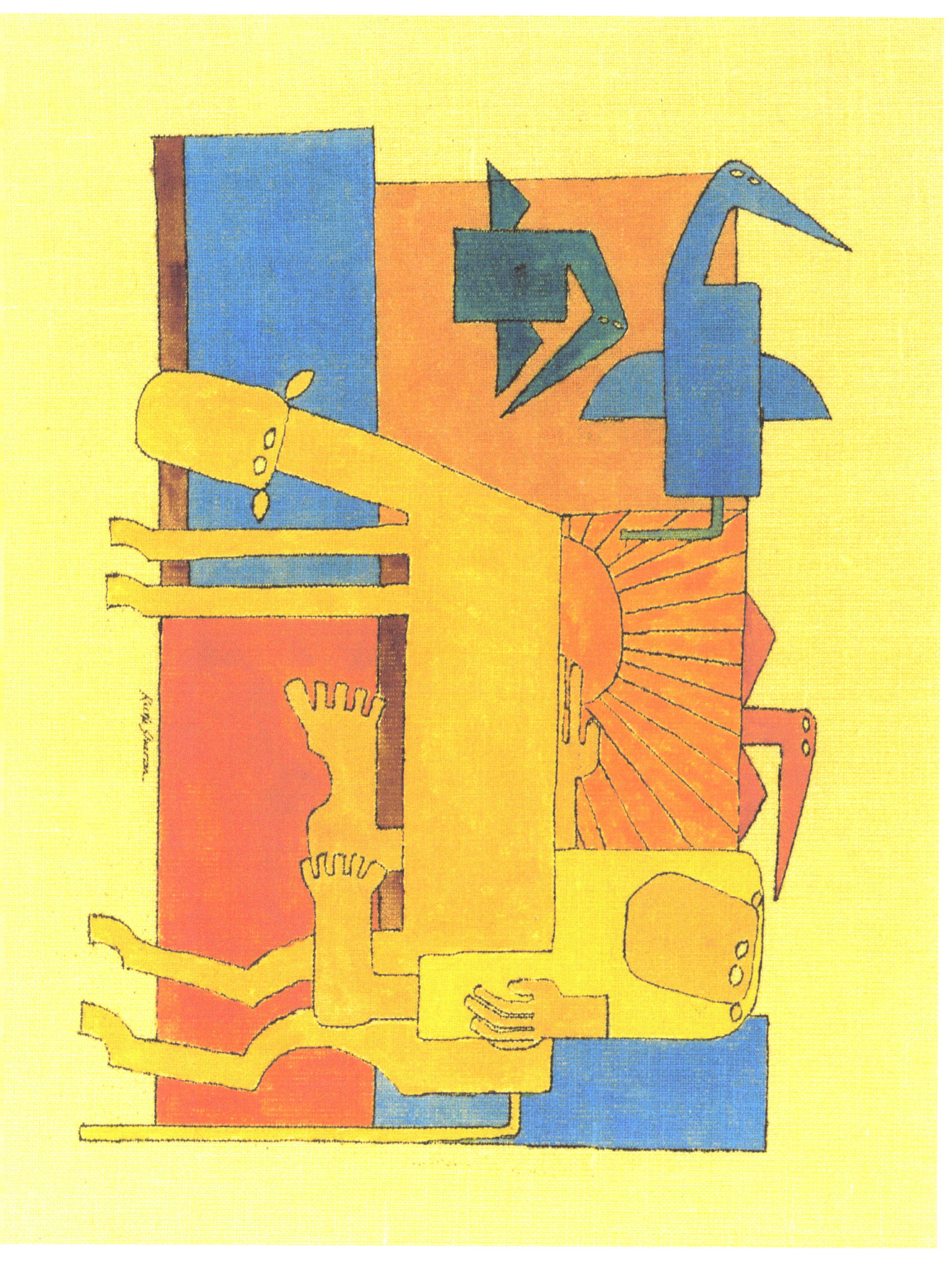

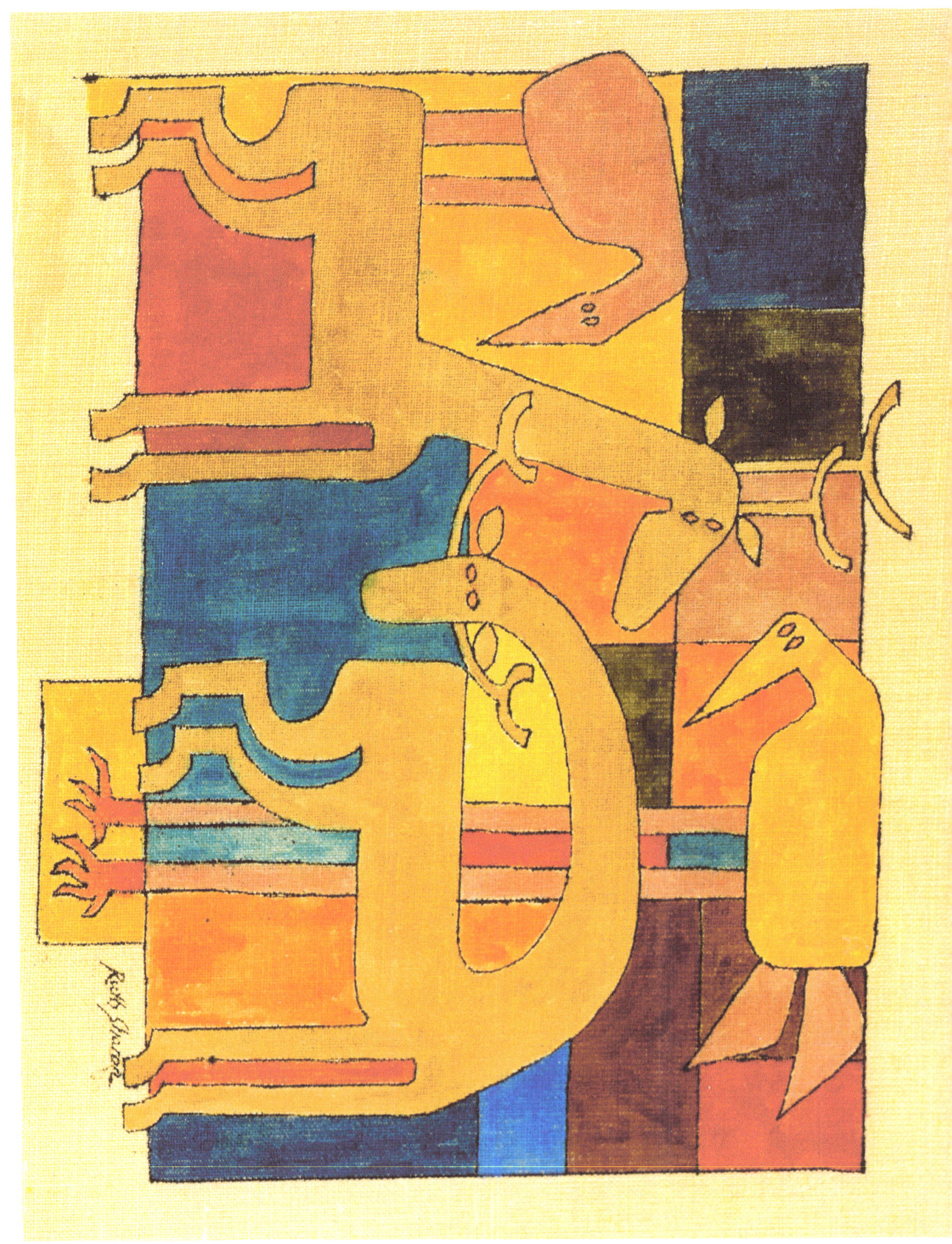

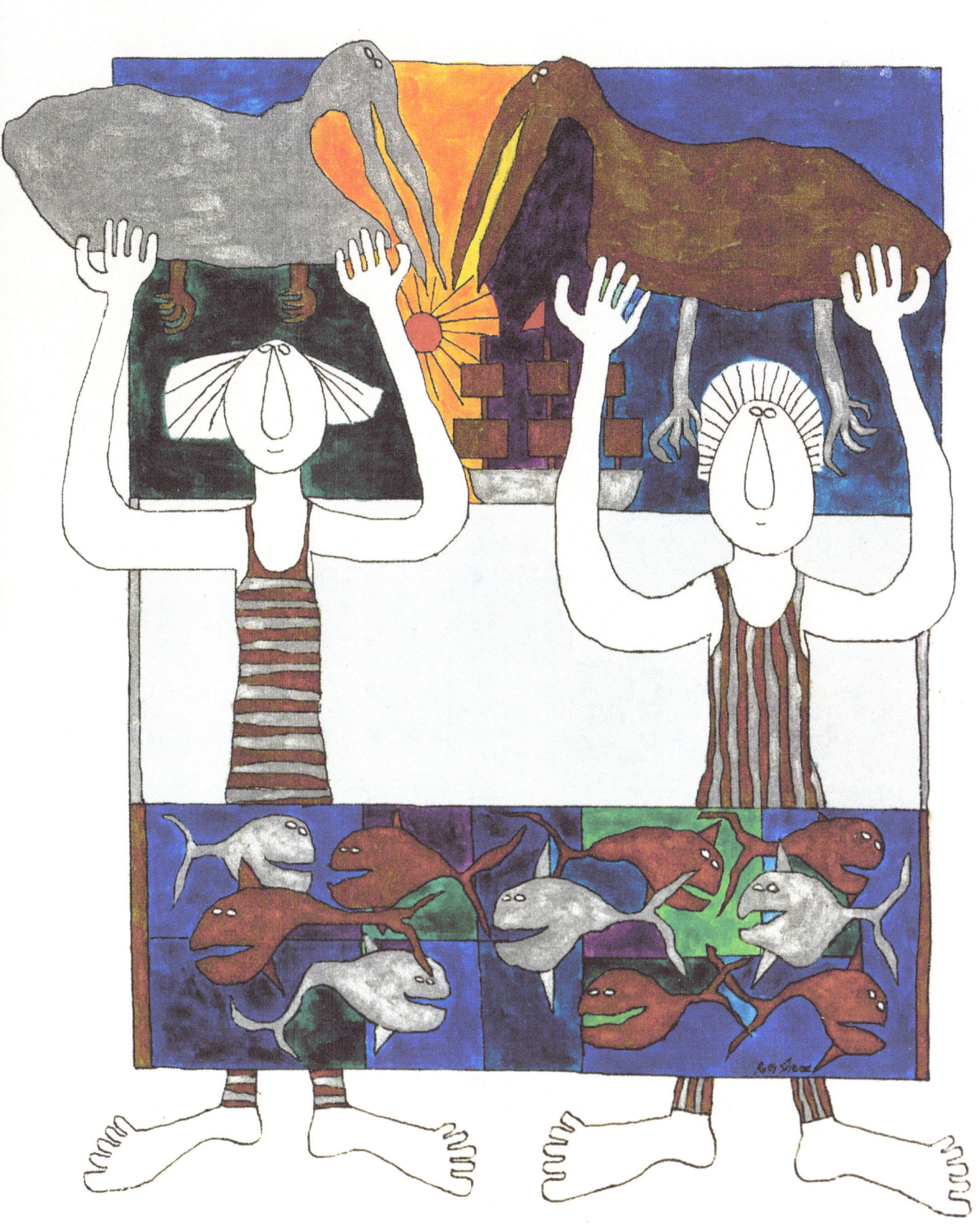

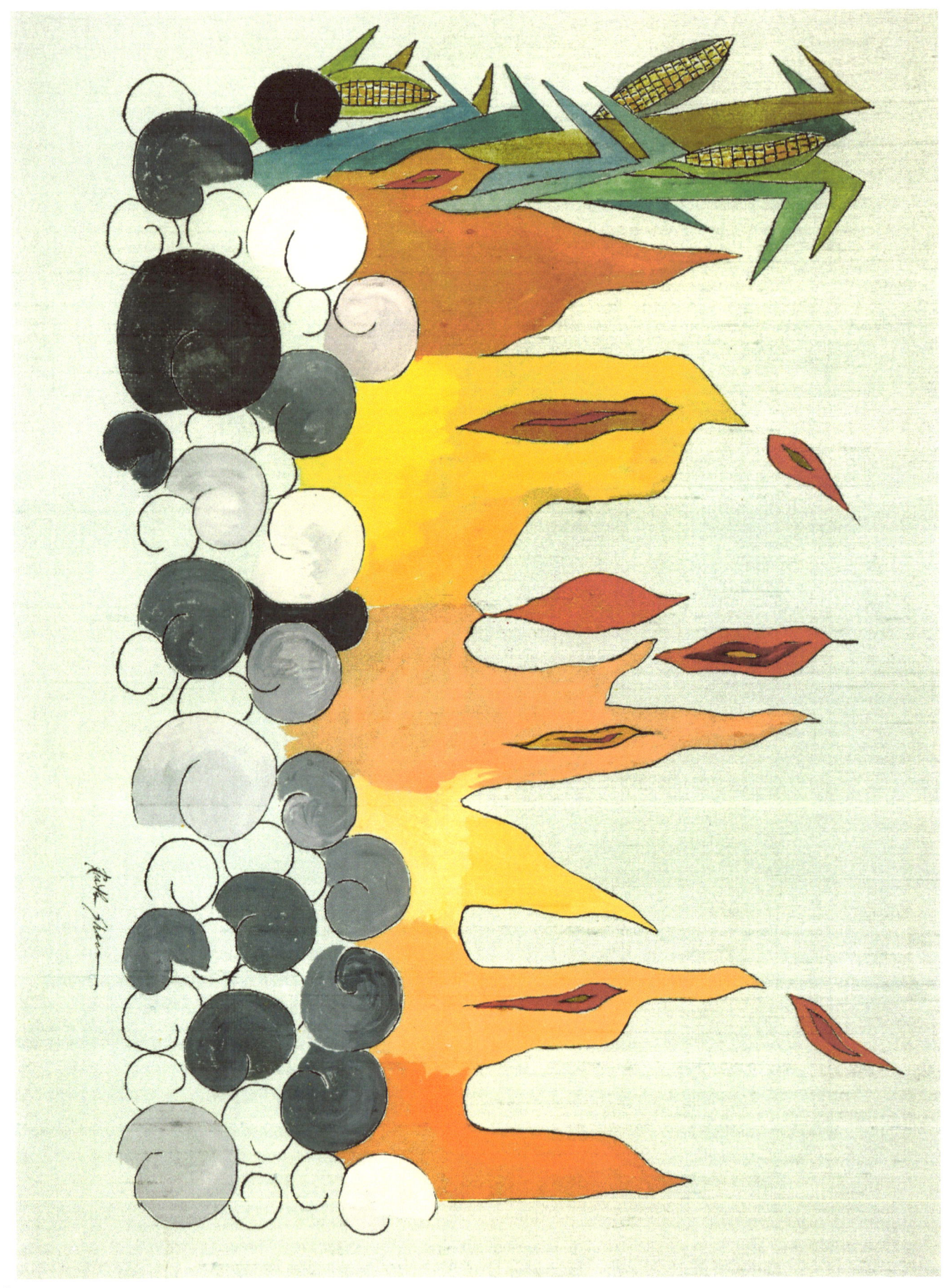

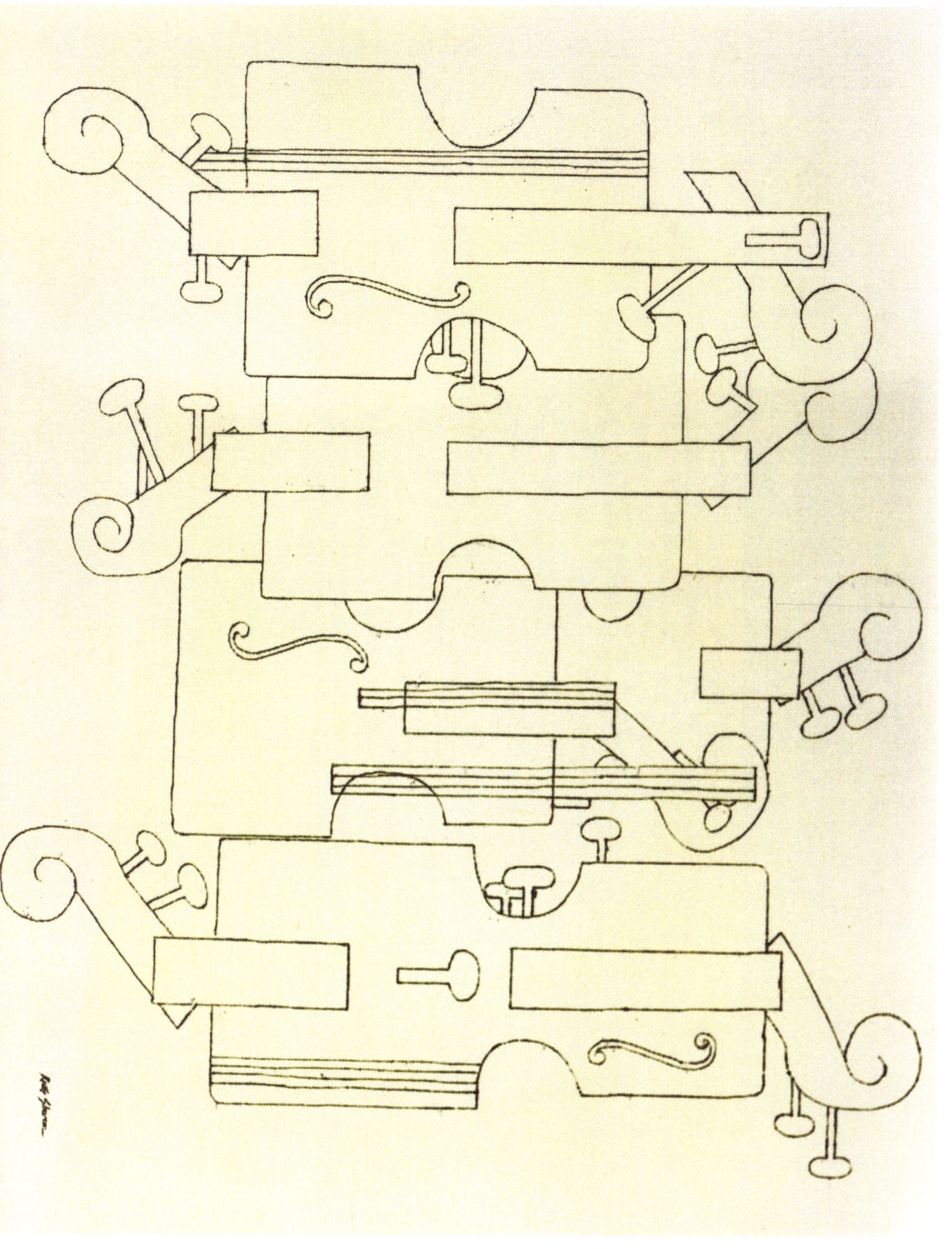

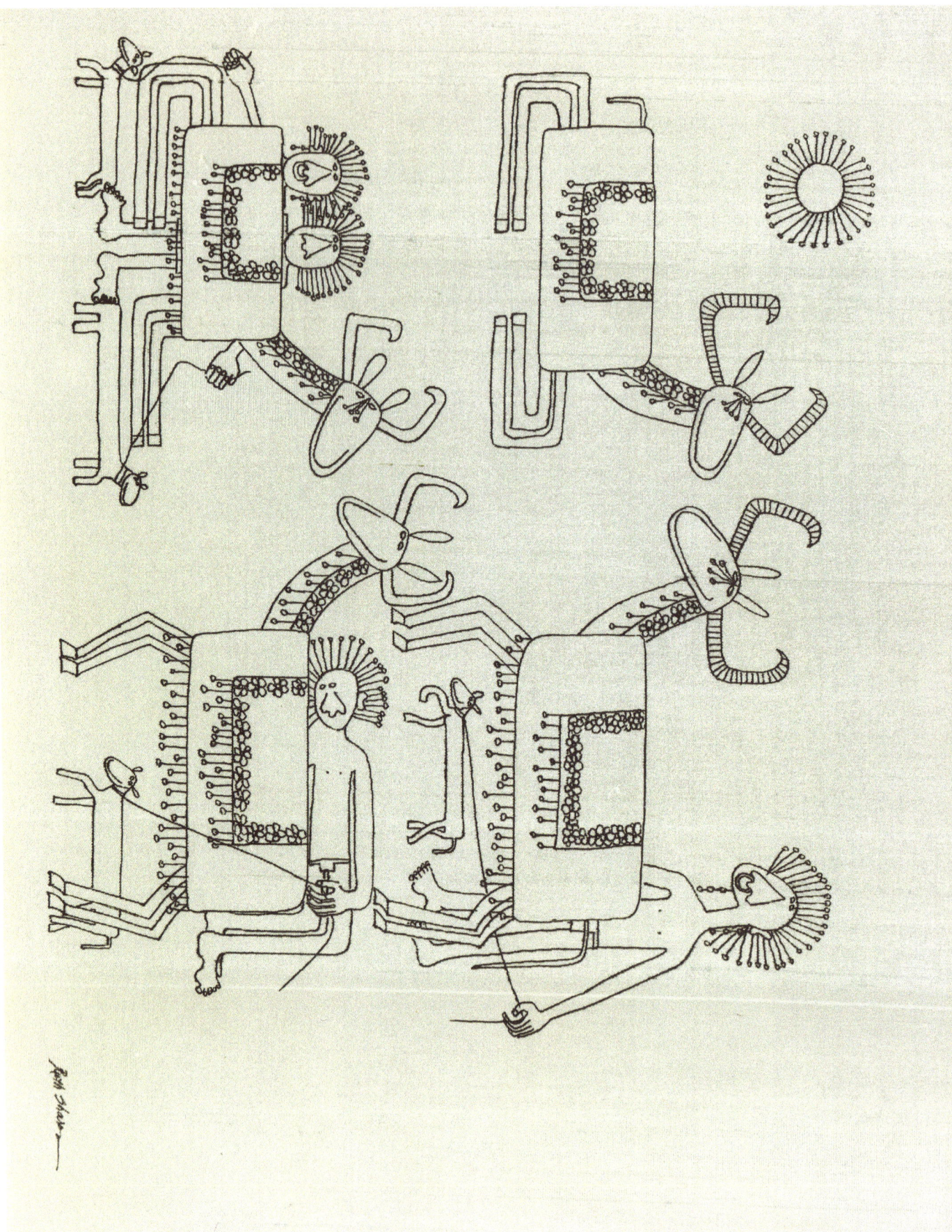

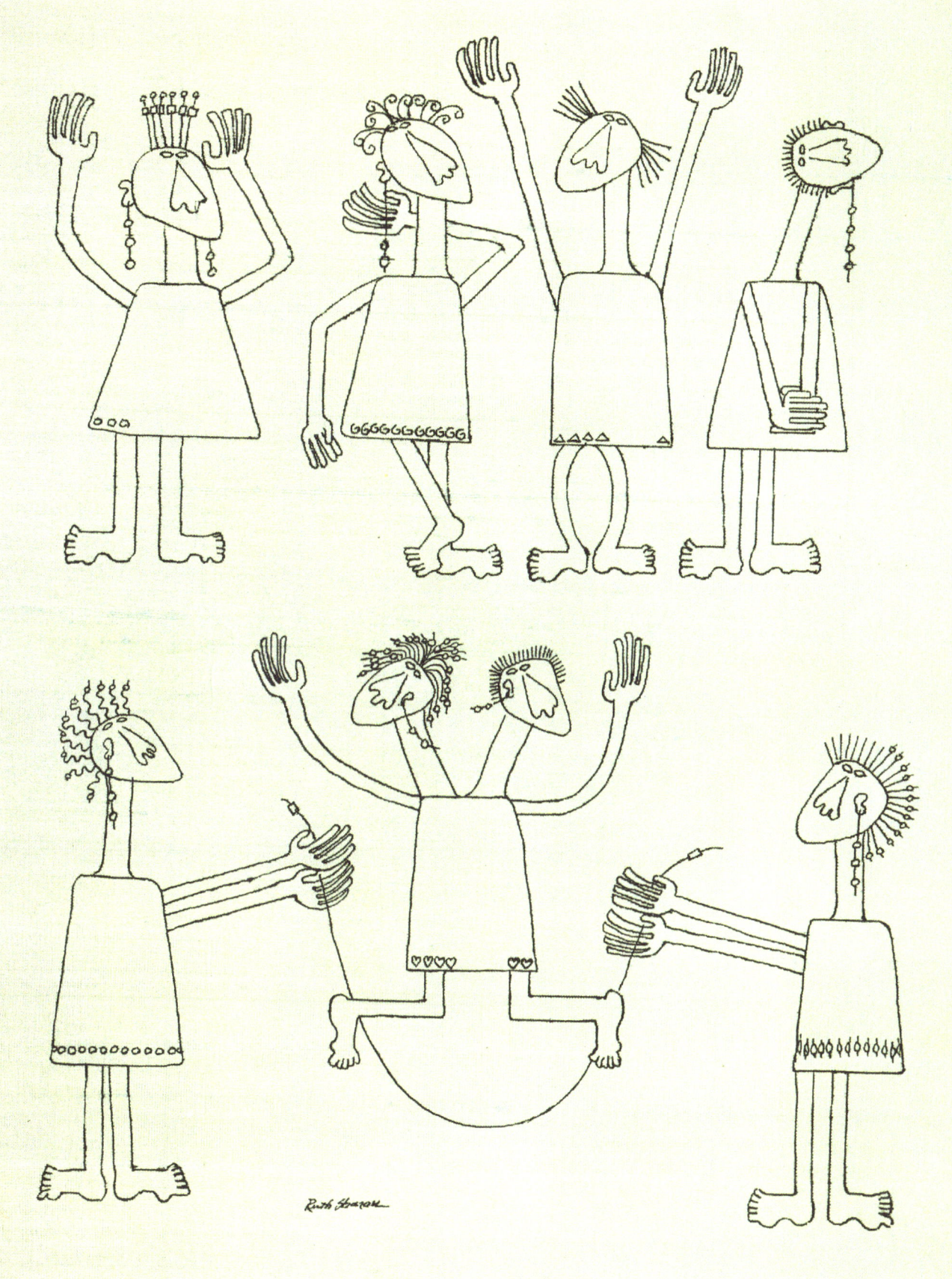

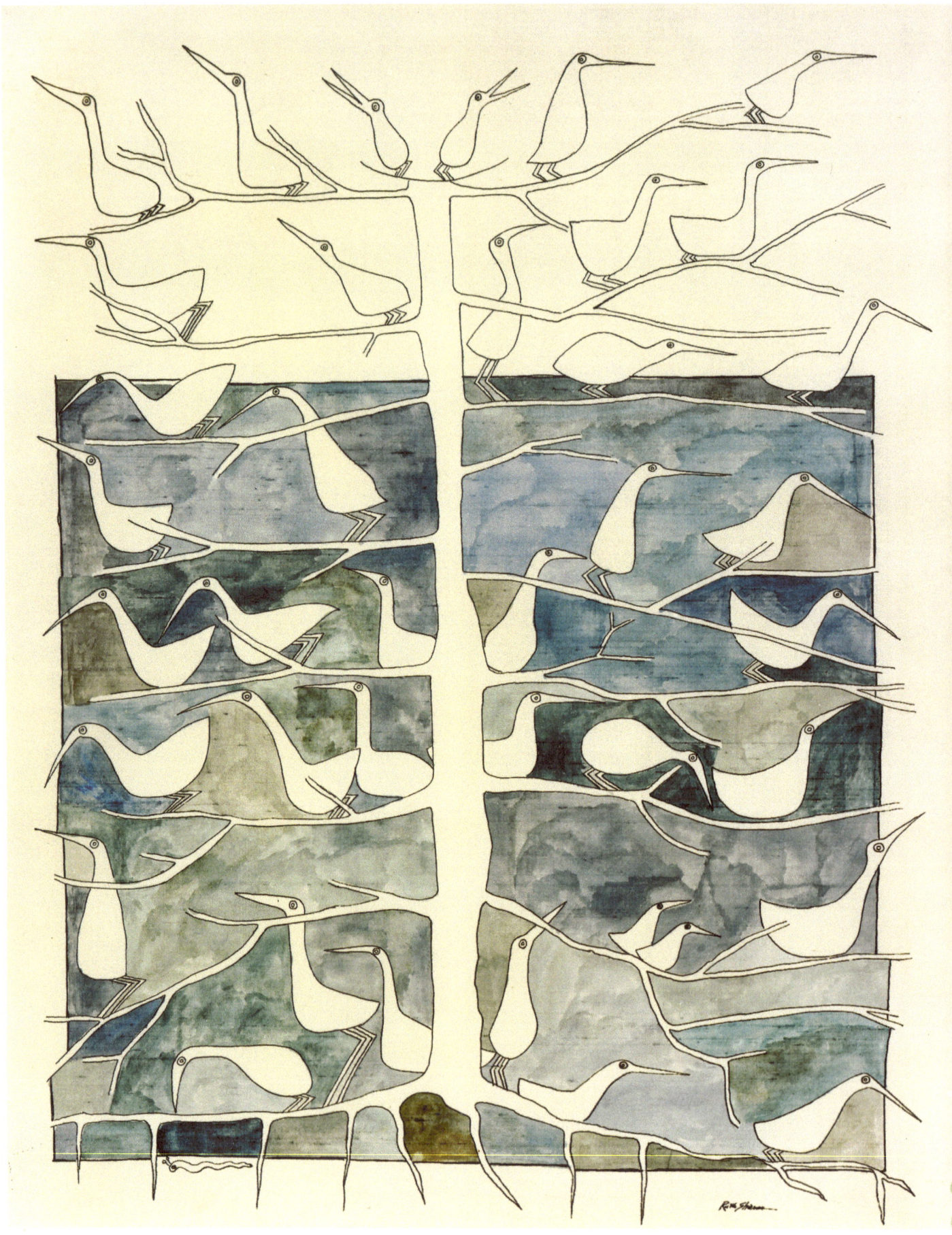

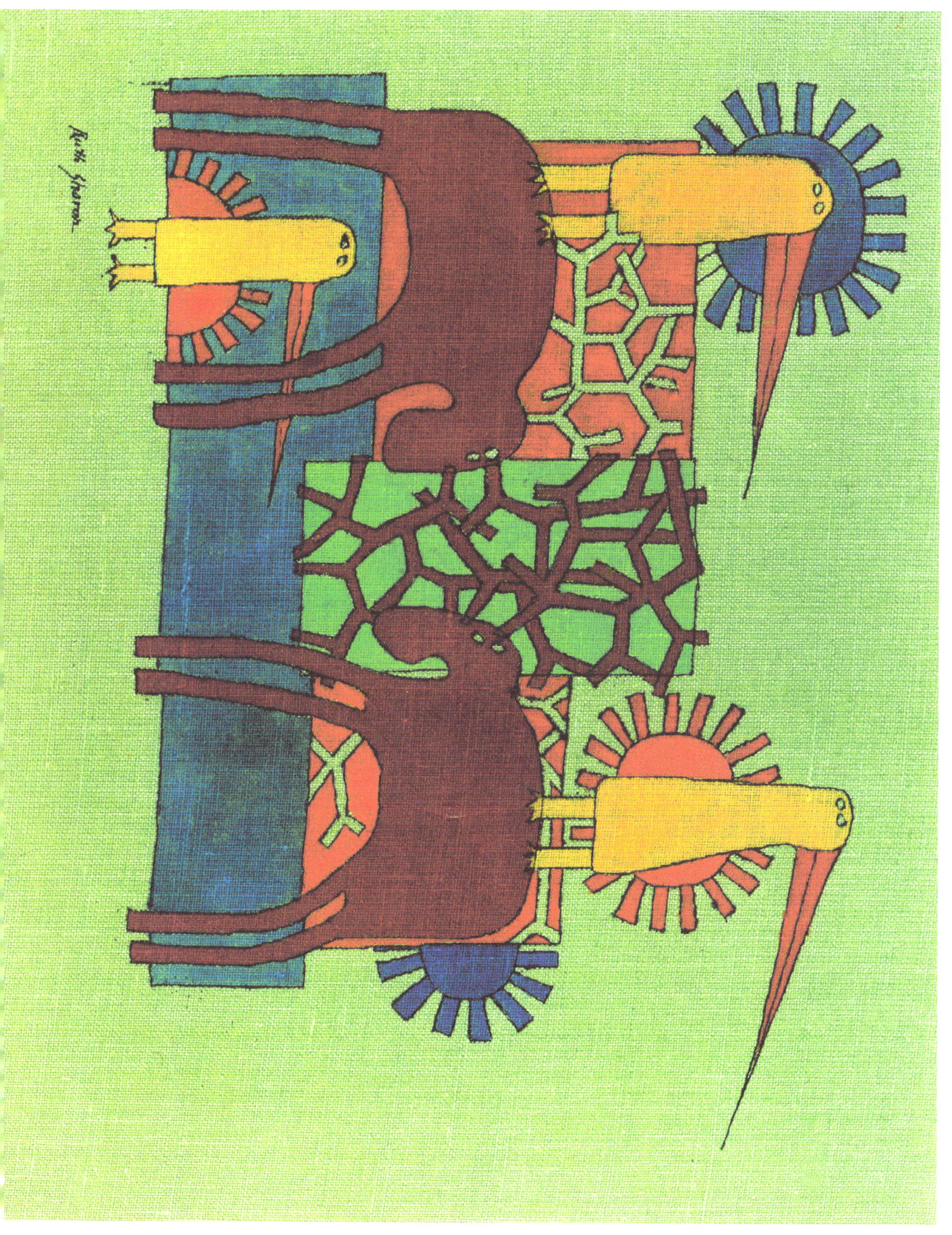

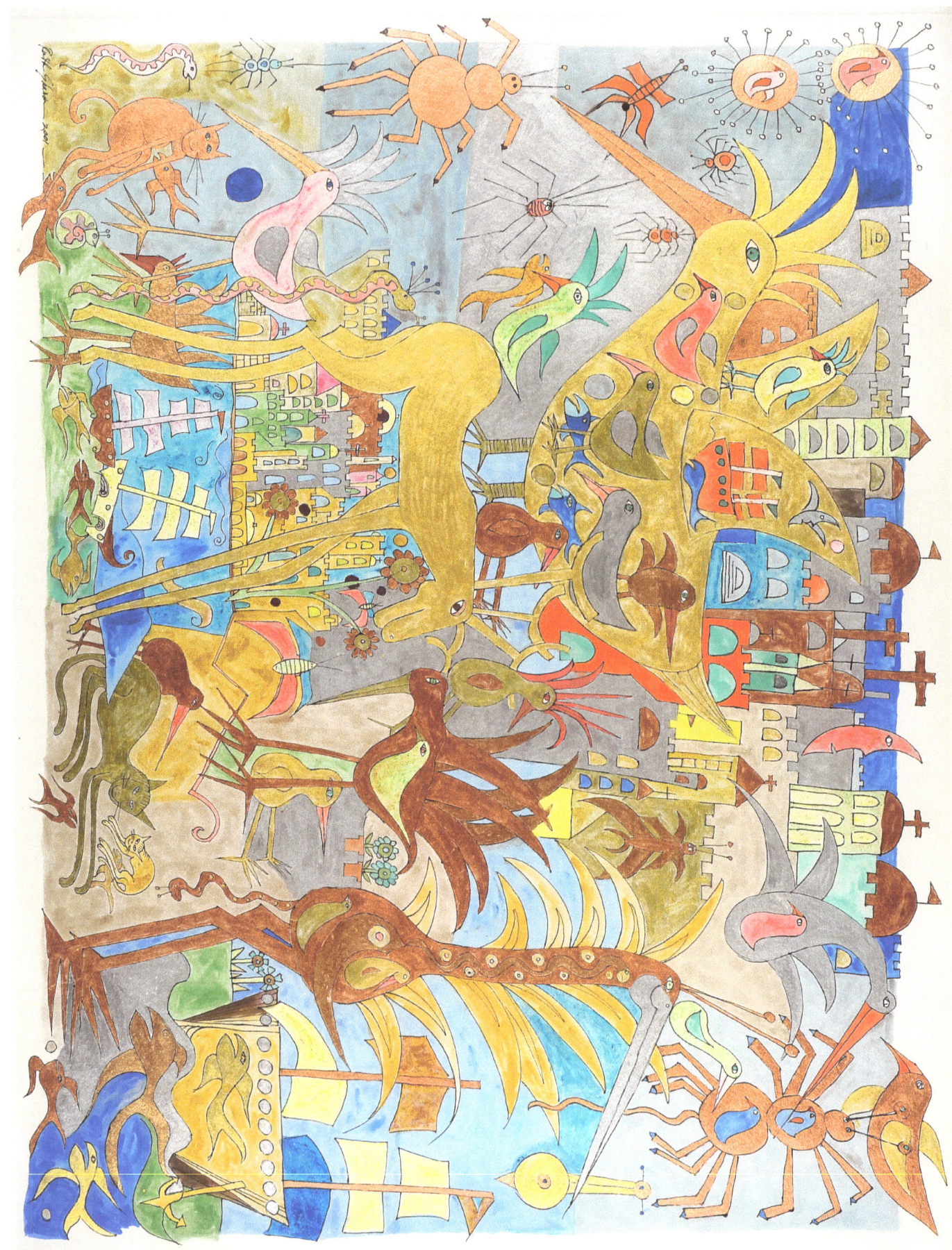

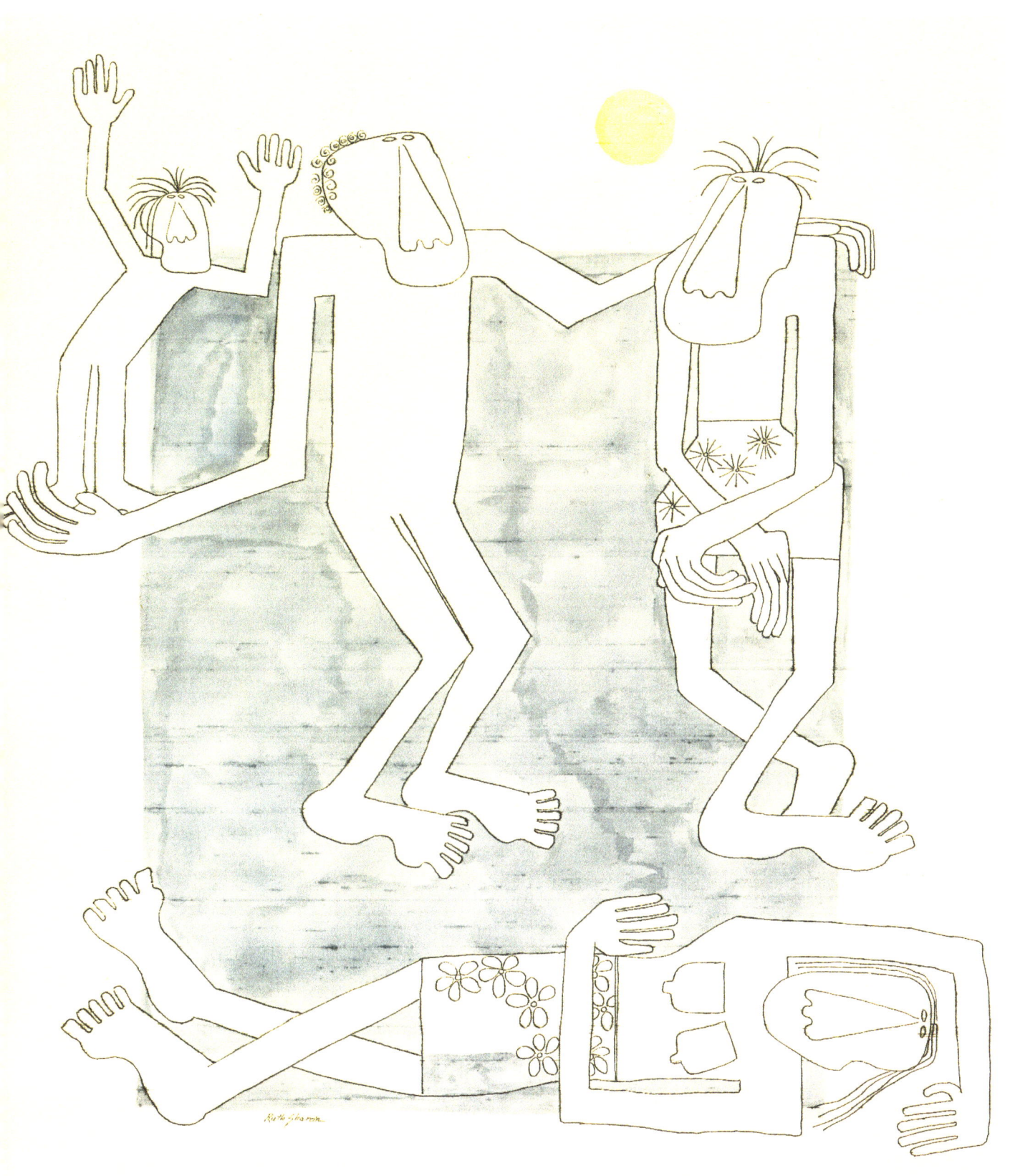

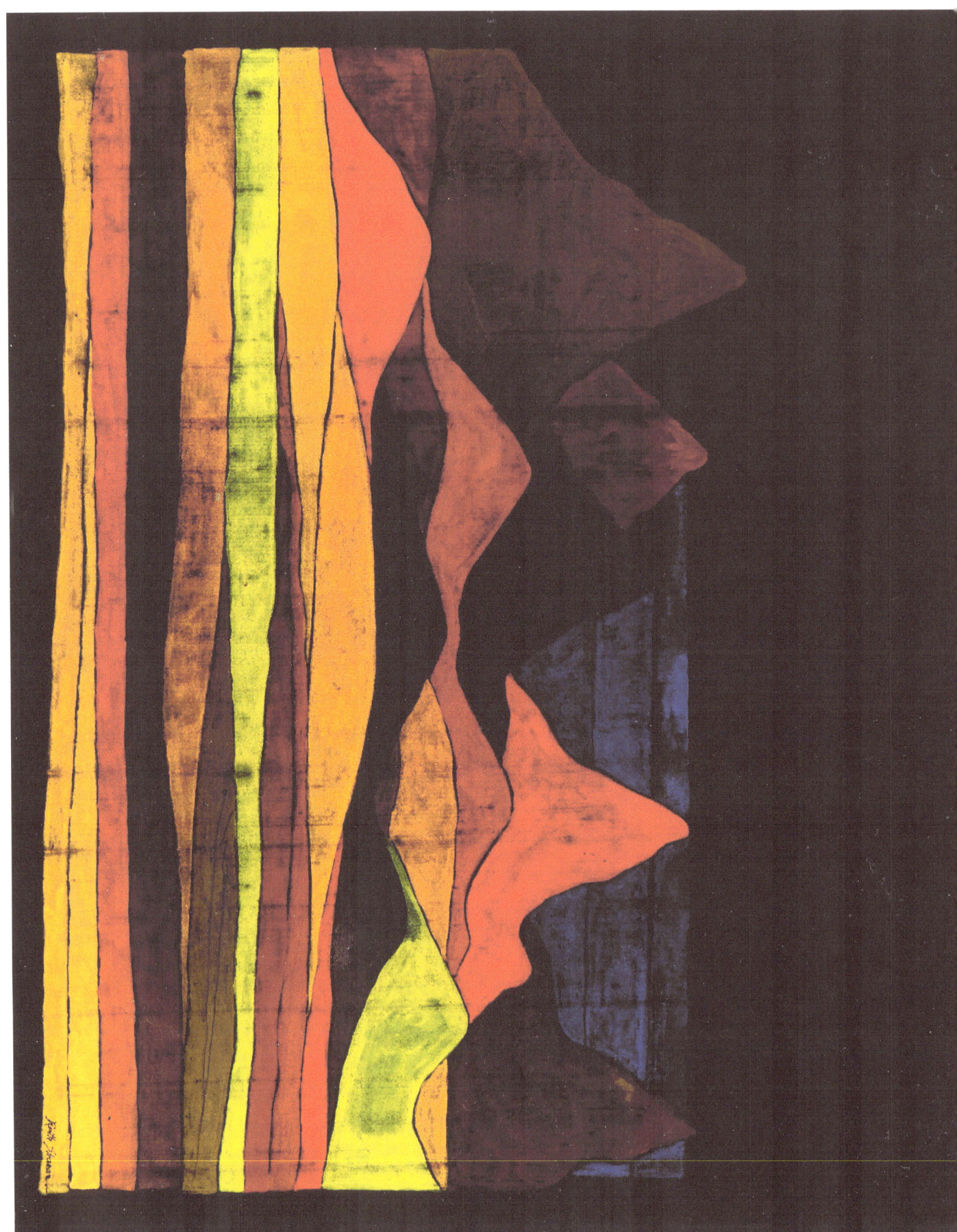

ABA - The Glory and the Torment

by Ruth Velikovsky Sharon, PhD

ISBN 978-1-906833-20-6

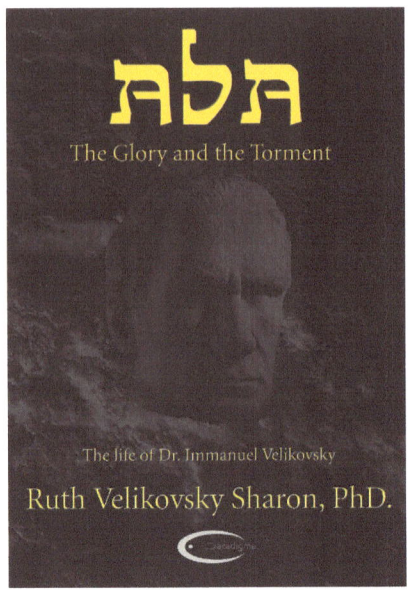

In this book you get to know Immanuel Velikovsky as a person. His daughter Ruth describes his childhood, his family environment and his eventful life.

Using plenty of background information, numerous anecdotes and many photographs she makes us familiar with her father, but also shows the personal dimension of the devastating campaign he encountered to in the last decades of his life.

The Truth Behind the Torment

by Ruth Velikovsky Sharon, PhD

ISBN 978-1-906833-21-3

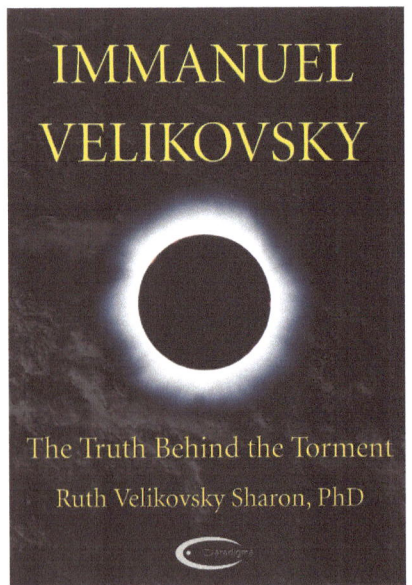

In this supplement to her father's biography, Ruth Velikovsky Sharon, PhD. depicts the true facts about the campaign against him.

She publishes revealing letters in full length, that show the true nature of the undeserving - unscientific - treatment of Velikovsky by the scientific establishment, a treatment that appears rather medieval than enlightened.

Shame on You - You Were in My Dream

by Ruth Velikovsky Sharon, PhD

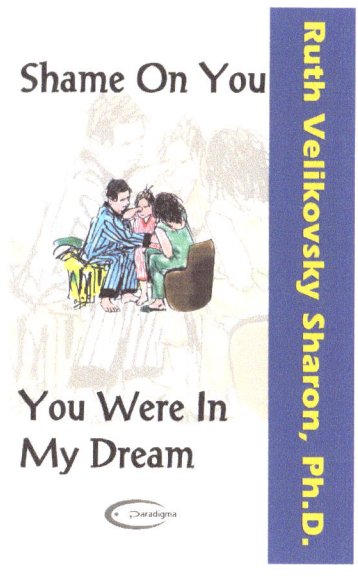

ISBN 978-1-906833-01-5

Finally a new and easy guide to the understanding of dreams, which really makes sense!
Ruth Velikovsky Sharon, PhD has developed a completely new understanding of the nature of dreams, which is fascinating because of its simplicity and its practical orientation.

She questions ideas we have long taken for granted. She asks us to reconsider what the word "dream" really means. She shows us that to use the word "dream" in partnership with "He is a dreamboat" or "My dream house!" is to misuse or even abuse the word "dream".
In her book, Dr. Sharon describes the way that parents can be of help vis a vis dreams: Listen and Learn. Ask your children how they felt in the dream, ask them what they thought in the dream.
She includes chapters on manipulation in dreams, dream catchers and other gadgets and the environment and dreams.
Also included is a reprint of the article "A New Understanding of Dreams", published by Dr. Sharon in *New Jersey Medicine*, Journal of the Medical Society of New Jersey, January 1995 issue.

The More You Explain - The Less They Understand

by Ruth Velikovsky Sharon, PhD and John Cathro Seed, MD

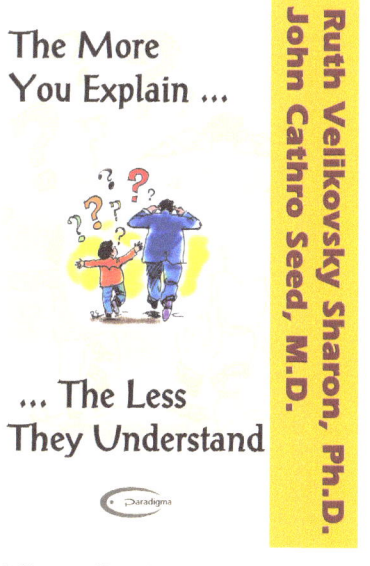

ISBN 978-1-906833-00-8

In this, perhaps the most encompassing of her works, Dr. Ruth Velikovsky Sharon brilliantly lifts the veil that shrouds the mystery of psychoanalysis, revealing intrinsic truths that can forever assist us in our journey to self-discovery and growth.
Like a finely tuned and well-trained instrument, Dr. Sharon makes her probe into the human psyche sound easy - resulting in a compilation of luminous insights that are warm in their humanity, vibrant in their simplicity, and even touched with humor.

Harvard Medical School trained, Dr. John C. Seed's contribution of the Physical Health chapter will enlighten the medical community as well as the average reader, and if abided by, will help prolong life.

www.ingramcontent.com/pod-product-compliance
Lightning Source LLC
Chambersburg PA
CBHW051154220526
45473CB00003B/766